THE NewStar GUIDE TO CELEBRITY HOMES

LOS ANGELES

THE NewStar GUIDE TO CELEBRITY HOMES

LOS ANGELES

by Bruce W. Cook

The sale of this book without its cover is unauthorized.
If you purchased this book without a cover, you should be
aware that it was reported to the publisher as "unsold and
destroyed." Neither the author nor the publisher has
received payment for the sale of this "stripped book."

Copyright © 1998 by Bruce Cook

All rights reserved. No part of this book may be
reproduced or transmitted in any form or by any means,
electronic or mechanical, including photocopying,
recording, or by any information storage and retrieval
system, without permission in writing from the publisher.

ISBN: 0-7871-1770-6

NewStar Press
a division of NewStar Media Inc.
8955 Beverly Boulevard
Los Angeles, CA 90048

Cover design by Rick Penn-Kraus
Text design and layout by Michele Lanci-Altomare
with Heather Parlato
Maps by Publishers' Art
Printed by Wright Color Graphics

First NewStar Press Trade Paperback Printing:
November 1998

10 9 8 7 6 5 4 3 2 1

Printed in the United States of America

Acknowledgments

Special thanks to the following individuals who assisted
in the research and compilation of information
that made this book possible: JoAnn Dean Killingsworth,
Joleen Parham, Meg Flemion, Dora Zuniga, Emily Barber,
and Alexandra Blaire Cook. And heartfelt appreciation to
Angela Poursalimi, Kevin Vandershans, and Pepper Hollingsworth,
Equity Title Company, for their professional "fact-finding" input.

Contents

A Note Before You Begin...................*xiii*
Introduction ....*xv*

Chapter One **2**
Los Angeles
From the West Adams district south of downtown, where turn-of-the-century stars such as Fatty Arbuckle, Theda Bara, and Norma Talmadge resided in the dream homes of the 1910s era, to Hancock Park in the Central Wilshire Corridor of Los Angeles, where the new Hollywood of the 1920s moved in on old Los Angeles society.

Chapter Two **14**
Hollywood
Founded in the latter part of the nineteenth century by very proper Midwestern evangelists, Hollywood did not welcome the invasion of show business. However, these visionaries did not let the conservative nature of the early residents prevent them from building the first studios as well as homes for the stars of this new medium—the movies. On Sunset and Hollywood Boulevards, stretching to Whitley Heights on the east and Fairfax on the west, Hollywood features the homes of Bette Davis, Louis B. Mayer, Houdini...as well as Madonna, Nicolas Cage, and Jerry Seinfeld.

Hollywood Hills

Many stars have migrated from the flats of Hollywood to seek privacy in the verdant hills. As their careers rose, so did the residences in the hills. From Beechwood Canyon in the east, to Sunset Plaza in the west, visit the hillside homes of David Schwimmer, Orson Welles, and Matthew Perry.

West Hollywood

A small enclave of what is today mostly multiunit housing. West Hollywood sits in a valuable triangle of land between Beverly Hills, Hollywood, and the Wilshire Corridor. It always had a rather artistic and bohemian air, and in the early days attracted the likes of F. Scott Fitzgerald, Errol Flynn, and Cary Grant. Today, West Hollywood's mixture of culture, class, and lifestyle runs the spectrum from a constantly shifting immigrant population to an active gay and lesbian contingent to a rebel class of young stars.

Chapter Three 30

Beverly Hills—The Flats

The name of Beverly Hills has meant star homes ever since Mary Pickford and Douglas Fairbanks built their once remote hunting lodge known as Pickfair in the hills of Benedict Canyon. Part of the Beverly Hills star tour concentrates on "the flats" of Beverly Hills. "The flats" are simply the streets of handsome residences between Santa Monica Boulevard on the southern border, Sunset Boulevard on the northern border, Doheny Drive to the west, and Whittier Drive to the east.

From classics such as James Cagney, Spencer Tracy, Eddie Cantor, Charlie Chaplin, and Clark Gable to contemporaries the likes of Phil Collins, Faye Dunaway, and Smokey Robinson, Beverly Hills is America's dreamland of celebrity real estate.

The Hills

North of Sunset Boulevard, from major estates to canyon hideaways, the "North of Sunset" crowd includes everyone from Ann-Margret and Don Johnson to Eddie Murphy and James Woods.

Beverly Hills Post Office

They still have a Beverly Hills address, even though these stars live in cities such as Sherman Oaks and Los Angeles. This is the high hill country surrounding the ridge known the world over as Mulholland Drive, and served by the Beverly Hills Post Office, hence the address. Watch the curves and narrow roads as you track down the homes of Jack Nicholson, Warren Beatty, Magic Johnson, and Wayne Gretzky.

Chapter Four 74
Bel Air

The Beverly Hillbillies actually lived in Bel Air, and so have Charles Bronson, Tom Cruise, Ryan O'Neal, Farrah Fawcett, Clint Eastwood, Peter Fonda, and Elizabeth Taylor. Tour some of the most beautiful hillside homes in America, all built in the canyons beyond the gates on Sunset Boulevard erected by 1920s real estate visionary Alphonso Bell.

Chapter Five 90
Holmby Hills

Perhaps the most costly residential neighborhood in all the world, Holmby Hills is located in a small canyon area between Beverly Hills to the east, Westwood to the west, and Bel Air to the north. With celebrity homes ranging in cost from a low of around $2 million for a fixer-upper to more than $75 million, get ready to drop your jaw as you survey the abodes of Hugh Hefner, Aaron Spelling, Henry Mancini, and more.

Westwood and Century City

From quaint Spanish bungalows to colonials designed by celebrity architect Paul Williams in the heyday of Los Angeles residential development, to the new high-rise condos of the Wilshire Corridor and Century City, Westwood is home to Carol Burnett, Tom Selleck, and Toni Braxton.

Chapter Six 106
Brentwood

Quiet (at least until O.J. Simpson moved in), ultraexclusive, and with a decidedly lower profile than Beverly Hills and Bel Air to the east, Brentwood has a bit of horsey flair—English saddle horsey, that is. Actually, the only horses in Brentwood are found in Sullivan Canyon, a woodsy stretch of road off Mandeville Canyon (just north of Sunset Boulevard) that is home to many stars, including Robert Wagner and Jill St. John, Harrison Ford, and Gregory Peck. The rest of Brentwood is quite formal and traditional, with an emphasis on green space and privacy.

Marilyn Monroe, Steve McQueen, Tom Hanks, Jim Belushi, Michael Douglas, and James Garner have called Brentwood home.

Chapter Seven....................124
Pacific Palisades

The rustic coastal hills of the Pacific Palisades is the destination du jour for a great percentage of young Hollywood. The clean air, the views of mountains and ocean, and the atmosphere of relaxed California chic, which was home to Ronald and Nancy Reagan from the sixties through Reagan's presidency, is home base for Bill Cosby, Billy Crystal, Arnold Schwarzenegger, and Goldie Hawn and Kurt Russell.

Chapter Eight 138
Santa Monica

Oh, to live by the sea. Santa Monica is an old town by Los Angeles standards, dating back to the mid-nineteenth century and the founding of California. In the 1920s William Randolph Hearst built a palace by the sea for his mistress, actress Marion Davies, on the Santa Monica shoreline known as the Gold Coast. Today, contemporary Hollywood prefers Gillette Regent Square, a rather traditional neighborhood of mostly old and handsome homes built in rows on flat streets leading to the edge of the Pacific Ocean. Mel Brooks and Anne Bancroft, Jeff Bridges, Sylvester Stallone, and Jamie Lee Curtis all call Santa Monica home sweet home.

Chapter Nine..................... 146
Malibu

Playground in the sand for the rich, the divorced, the rehabilitated, or soon-to-be rehabilitated, the glory of Malibu attracts the biggest, the best, the brightest, the brashest, and the everything to anyone who can afford life by the water. Fires, floods, earthquakes, traffic, and real estate taxes can't keep them away. Barbra Streisand, Cher, Jackie Collins, Michael Jackson, recently split Pamela Anderson and Tommy Lee, Nick Nolte, and Sean Penn are among the Hollywood contingent encamped in Malibu.

Chapter Ten...................... 172
The Valley

Sherman Oaks, Encino, and Studio City are home to countless entertainment personalities, including Tiffani-Amber Thiessen, John Travolta, David Hasselhoff, and Cuba Gooding Jr.

The East San Fernando Valley

Studios and stars mingle in Van Nuys, North Hollywood, Toluca Lake, and Burbank. From Bob Hope to Denzel Washington to Andy Garcia, the East Valley has its own particular lifestyle and feeling.

The West San Fernando Valley

Horses, hills, public schools with high standards, family values, and a bit of land attract David Hasselhoff, Patrick Swayze and John Ratzenberger.

Index........................ 189

A Note Before You Begin

ALL OF THE INFORMATION CONTAINED IN THIS book comes from the public records. There is no guesswork, and none of the facts is based on inside information or third-party information of any kind. It is important to note that the public record offers a disclaimer "that the information sourced from public documents is not guaranteed." In other words, even the records kept by the government and used for taxes and title on everyone's property in the state of California may not be 100 percent accurate.

It is also important to note that celebrities move faster than many of us can change the bed. We have made a considerable effort to distinguish between present and former addresses of the stars in this book. However, it is possible that some of your favorites may not live in the house listed by the time this book gets in your hands. Further, it is also possible that some of the star real estate has transferred between parties, been torn down, burned down, moved off the lot, or removed by forces of nature.

This guide is meant to entertain and should not be used as gospel in relation to the real estate information provided, although best efforts were made to obtain accurate and timely facts. In cases where present market value is provided, the figures represent an educated estimate based on comparable sales figures in the area at the time of publication. Formal inspections and quantitative and qualitative property analysis have not been done on subject properties. Therefore, projections of real market value are only projections, and while they are based on expert judgment, they are not meant to be taken as irrefutable fact.

In this age of information we respectfully request that you honor the privacy of the celebrities listed in this guide. Try to imagine what it would be like to have your address listed for all the world to read, and remember, many of these homes are occupied by new, non-celebrity owners just like yourself. Climbing over walls is strictly forbidden, even if Lucille Ball did it in one of her "I Love Lucy" episodes to get a better look at William Holden. But there's no law against taking a picture of your favorite star's home, or even asking for an autograph if you're lucky enough to pass by when one of them is walking the dog. Yes, they do have dogs, and some of them really walk them.

This is the most complete guide to star real estate in Los Angeles. Enjoy the adventure.

Introduction

PEOPLE ARE CURIOUS. WHAT ARE THE FIRST questions asked of you when you meet a stranger? "What do you do?" and "Where do you live?" Now if you happen to be a movie star and live in Beverly Hills, the curiosity factor grows exponentially. Actually, ever since the beginning of motion pictures back in the early part of this century, the founding fathers of filmed entertainment were of the opinion that stars needed to live like stars. As nickel ticket sales turned into millions of dollars in profits, the stars found plenty of reasons to live in grandeur. It is a tradition that flourished through the 1920s and 1930s, despite a crippling depression felt the world over. And it was revitalized in the postwar fifties and sixties, and boomed in the 1980s. The minimalist 90s have not diminished the trend, only redefined it. The new adage is simply that less costs more.

From the first footprint that hit the cement of Walter Grauman's Chinese Theatre, the fans of the stars clamored to know every detail about their lives. Shoe size was just the tip of the iceberg. What says more about a person than their home? And when it comes to stars, the homes, for the most part, then and now, are illustrations of their characters. Manifestations of their dreams. And our dreams as well. For many generations of Americans, the saying "to live like a star", meant to live like royalty in a very uniquely American sense of the expression.

While our feelings and relationships with our stars are decidedly different than those of our parents' and grandparents' time, people are still curious about the real lives of the folks we know so well on screen. And it's not just seeing the house that counts; we want to know the facts. So, in addition to the names and the addresses, *The NewStar Guide to Celebrity Homes* is going to present you with information such as the size of the home, the price paid, the taxes, the number of bathrooms, and more. Now do you really need to know how many bathrooms Goldie Hawn has in her Pacific Palisades home? She has twelve, according to title records. See, now that was something you wouldn't know just driving by.

Each chapter of *The NewStar Guide to Celebrity Homes* is meant to give the reader (the looker or the driver) an easy do-it-yourself insider's tour of the vast celebrity real estate of Los Angeles. From the Adams district south of downtown to the Malibu Colony and the San Fernando Valley, *The NewStar Guide to Celebrity Homes* will direct you, neighborhood by neighborhood. You'll be such an expert on star real estate you'll be able to get a California Real Estate License and go to work. Or maybe you'll just have the time of your life dreaming away as you explore the homes and habitats of your famous friends. When you go home, be sure to laud it over all of your family and friends that you not only know where Harrison Ford lives, you also know how much he paid in real estate taxes last year. And not only will you know the inside scoop on your favorite movie or TV star. *The NewStar Guide to Celebrity Homes* will also take you to the homes of many famous individuals in the areas of sports, fashion, business, music, politics, and more.

One very important caveat. All of the information in this celebrity guide is personal. None of it is secret. It is all a matter of public record. However, while the price of fame does mean a loss of privacy when it comes to public information, it should not mean an invitation to intrude on the premises of the stars you love and want to know more about. This book is not in any way meant to be an invitation to climb over the fence of Arnold Schwarzenegger's home. Be respectful of the privacy and the property of those you are about to check out.

It's a free country, and the information contained herein is meant to entertain. Use it accordingly, and have a marvelous star tour in the City of Angels. Who knows, maybe it's your dream someday to live like a star. And maybe, that dream will come true.

THE NewStar GUIDE TO CELEBRITY HOMES

LOS ANGELES

Chapter One

Los Angeles

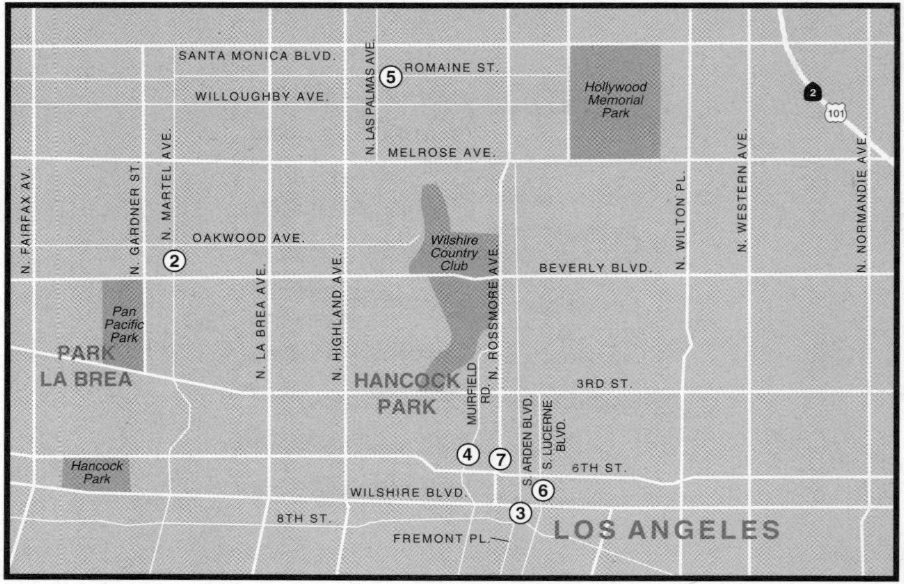

1. FATTY ARBUCKLE, THEDA BARA, RAOUL WALSH, MIRIAM COOPER, JOE SCHENCK, & NORMA TALMADGE/649 West Adams Blvd.
2. DREW BARRYMORE/360 N. Martel Ave.
3. ANGELA BASSETT/69 Fremont Place
4. NAT "KING" COLE/401 S. Muirfield Rd.
5. BUDDY EBSEN/1040 North Las Palmas Ave.
6. JOHN MALKOVICH/346 S. Lucerne Blvd.
7. MAE WEST/570 N. Rossmore Ave.

IN THE EARLY DAYS OF FILM, ITS stars—Chaplin, Keaton, West, Pickford, Fields, Talmadge, Valentino, Fairbanks, and Swanson—ushered in the "Jazz Age," not only for American fans of the growing cinema, but also for citizens worldwide. Movies changed the world much in the same way the combustible engine transformed the century. Nothing would ever be the same again.

Amid the reserved and dignified neighborhoods of Los Angeles, these stars of the cinema, who from the near get-go outearned the doctors and businessmen of their time, moved in and turned society upside down. The first neighborhood they invaded is known as the West Adams District, named for our early president, Adams, south of downtown Los Angeles off of the main avenue called Figueroa Street.

West Adams stretched for miles as Figueroa past the intersections of Hoover, Vermont, Arlington, and Crenshaw. This district was created in the 1980s when Methodist missionaries from the east and the midwest built the University of Southern California. At the turn of the century, this posh and respected district had mansions of the newly rich California barons lining West Adams for miles until the territory became uncharted.

The NewStar Guide to Celebrity Homes: Los Angeles

It was a perfect place to live for the new stars, young and brash and full of the promise their future held. They paid cash and moved into territory where "their kind" would have once been quite unwelcome by polite society. In a sense, the Hollywood invasion of West Adams could be labeled the first real estate takeover trend, the first in an ongoing series that have occurred in the City of Angels ever since.

Real estate in this city has depended on the fortunes, the trends, the lifestyles, and the attitudes of waves of inhabitants who have come here to seek opportunity. Consequently, the fate of West Adams began to turn as Hollywood moved in. Soon, the quiet neighborhood of sycamore- and elm-lined streets, boasting large Tudor, Elizabethan, and Italianate homes representing the exuberant taste and the popular architec-ture of the time, was inhabited by the likes of W.C. Fields and popular comic Fatty Arbuckle, who suffered a scandal involving a young girl that almost killed his career as surely as it killed the young woman.

The massive and elegant churches along West Adams buzzed with the locals' talk of their new neighbors. It wasn't long before the conservative rich of West Adams began to migrate west to newer neighborhoods known as Country Club Park, Windsor

Chapter One

Square, Hancock Park, Los Feliz, and Hollywoodland.

For those purists who want to see where the early stars called home, 649 West Adams beckons. This one house, at various times over a very short period of history, was home to the biggest names in entertainment at the time. The Tudor-style home still stands today, along with marvelous neighboring examples of the best that 1910 cinema dollars could buy in residential property.

After taking a look at West Adams between Figueroa and Hoover, continue to drive west on Adams and imagine that in 1910 this street was lined with the most beautiful homes in Southern California. Some remain, though most in decay, set between buildings, apartments, and various properties that defy most zoning experts' wildest imaginations. What you discover is a kaleidoscope of cultures and fortunes won and lost over decades of migration, a once glorious boulevard of dreams.

At Crenshaw, travel north and you pass through Country Club Park, a handsome section of mostly 1910 to 1920s-era homes of great style. To the north, across Wilshire Boulevard rests Hancock Park and Windsor Square, bordered by Wilton Place to the east and Highland Avenue to the west.

This spectacular enclave of architectural styles and verdant city gardens became the new West Adams in the late teens and early twenties. Home to the city's "old guard" for many decades, this area also became a celebrity stomping ground. Today many stars still live in and around Hancock Park, preferring its central city location and proximity to major studios such as Paramount Pictures on Melrose just to the north, and CBS Television City on Beverly Boulevard to the west. The old-world neighborhood feeling in Hancock Park remains today.

Many of the homes have incredible stories to tell. This was once the neighborhood of entertainment moguls such as Walt Disney and tycoons like Howard Hughes. Mae West lived here until her death. Young stars are now moving in, appreciating the value, the style, and the romance of old L.A.

Fatty Arbuckle
Theda Bara
Raoul Walsh
Miriam Cooper
Joe Schenck
Norma Talmadge

649 West Adams Boulevard
Los Angeles, CA 90007

THE FORMIDABLE TURN-OF-THE-CENTURY ENGLISH-STYLE home at 649 West Adams Boulevard was home to many of the screen's biggest names at a time when Los Angeles was just a small town busting at the seams—and housing was far from plentiful. Roscoe "Fatty" Arbuckle, one of the biggest names in early filmed slapstick comedy (at more than 266 pounds, he was in fact the biggest), lived in Hollywood rooming houses run by strict Christian landlords and ladies prior to residence in this version of the early movie star mansion. His wild behavior proved unpopular in the then very popular rooming house run by a woman named Miss Mara Hershey. Her 100-room establishment with sixty-six baths proved inadequate for Arbuckle. His fame and fortune enabled him to pick up and move to popular downtown Los Angeles, where the nightlife and the restaurants were much more in fashion. 649 West Adams would be the new address for the comic, who made a new movie almost every month with directors such as Mack Sennett, famous for the old Keystone Kops.

Arbuckle would be followed by Theda Bara, née Theodosia Goodman, the child of a tailor from Ohio, arguably one of the most famous of the early screen vixens.

She rocketed to international fame in 1917 with her portrayal of Cleopatra and became box office gold while in residence at the West Adams Boulevard address. Next, a young man named Raoul Walsh, a former fledgling silent screen actor who eventually found fame and fortune as a director, moved into West Adams with his bride, Miriam Cooper. A favorite actress of legendary director D.W. Griffith, Cooper portrayed Southern belle Margaret Cameron in the classic *The Birth of a Nation*.

Yet another Hollywood glamour couple would entertain residence at 649 West Adams. Producer Joe Schenck and his wife, Norma Talmadge, would make this abode home. Joe Schenck was no stranger to 649 West Adams in the society neighborhood known as Chester Place. He had worked with Fatty Arbuckle, making comedy shorts at Keystone Studios, and also with Theda Bara, making full-length films for the Comique Corporation. Later, Schenck was associated with the new Paramount Studios and was reportedly earning a four figure weekly salary. Talmadge was one of the big female box-office draws of the day, having appeared in more than a hundred films since her 1911 debut at the age of thirteen. Norma Talmadge was, by all reports, the most glamorous and the most eccentric of the West Adams residents. Apparently insurance companies of the day would not insure "movie people," so Talmadge garnered a reputation for hiding her jewels everywhere—from the icebox to the shoe racks of her closet—making sure that the colored stones corresponded to the appropriate color shoes in the closet.

Drew Barrymore 2

**360 N. Martel Avenue
Los Angeles, CA 90036**

THE ONETIME CHILD STAR, NOW AN INGENUE, IS A member of the famous Barrymore theatrical family. Drew Barrymore has chosen to live at a mid-Wilshire address, adjacent to Hancock Park and near the famous Farmer's Market on Fairfax Avenue. The *E.T.* co-star prefers simple digs, a three-bedroom, two-bath Spanish-style stucco home with pool, despite her success with films such as *Poison Ivy*, *Wayne's World 2*, *Boys on the Side*, *Batman Forever*, and *Ever After*.

YEAR BUILT: 1929
LOT SIZE: 8,250 SQ. FT.
ASSESSED VALUE: $416,400

Angela Bassett 3

**69 Fremont Place
Los Angeles, CA 90005**

THIS RISING FILM ACTRESS, WHO FIRST CAME TO prominence playing Tina Turner in the biopic *What's Love Got to Do With It?* lives in a gated community in the Hancock Park area just south of Wilshire Boulevard. Fremont Place, a small, elite community, was at one time the most elegant compound of estates in Los Angeles. Home to some of the city's wealthiest and most powerful residents, including at one time heavy-weight champion of the world, Muhammad Ali, Fremont Place, with its imposing concrete gates, is a favorite location spot for film companies. Angela Bassett's residence is a five-bedroom, six-bath home purchased in December 1994 for $1,030,000. Homes in Fremont Place sell for a low of $650,000 to more than $3 million.

YEAR BUILT: 1940
LOT SIZE: 27,225 SQ. FT.
HOME SIZE: 4,828 SQ. FT.

4 Nat "King" Cole

401 S. Muirfield Road
Los Angeles, CA 90020

THIS EXQUISITE ENGLISH TUDOR BRICK HOME ON A sweeping corner in Hancock Park attracted Nat "King" Cole, the first major black performer to star in his own network variety series (NBC, 1956-57). The singing star was at the peak of his career, with a young family, including a little girl named Natalie, to raise. When he purchased this residence in the 1950s, he broke the color barrier in this neighborhood. Today, the house would be worth more than $1.2 million. Built in 1924, the estate was sold to its present owner in 1974 for $250,002.

HOME SIZE: 6,809 SQ. FT.
LOT SIZE: 127,170 SQ. FT
ROOMS: 6 BEDROOMS, 5 BATHS

Chapter One

Buddy Ebsen 5

1040 North Las Palmas Avenue
Los Angeles, CA 90038

THE TALL, LANKY, VAUDEVILLIAN HOOFER CLAMPETT WHO became most famous as Uncle Jed Clampett on *The Beverly Hillbillies* television show (1962-71), once called Hancock Park home in the 1930s. Today Ebsen lives with his wife in Palos Verdes overlooking the Pacific, south of Los Angeles. During his heyday, Ebsen, who was the mild-mannered P.I. Barnaby Jones (1973-80) and Fess Parker's right-hand man in Disney's *Davy Crockett*, lived in this stately Los Angeles building while commuting to the studios.

John Malkovich 6

346 South Lucerne Boulevard
Los Angeles, CA 90020

CHILLING PERFORMANCES IN *THE KILLING FIELDS*, *Places in the Heart*, *Dangerous Liaisons*, and *In the Line of Fire* allow John Malkovich to live in a beautiful traditional home on tree-lined Lucerne Boulevard in the heart of Windsor Square. The Malkovich residence has four bedrooms and five baths. It was purchased in 1991 for $1,025,000.

YEAR BUILT: *1919*
LOT SIZE: *14,393 SQ. FT.*
HOME SIZE: *4,082 SQ. FT.*

7 Mae West

570 North Rossmore Avenue
Los Angeles, CA 90020

ONE OF THE STATELY BUILDINGS OF THE 1920S WAS home to siren Mae West until her death. Drive by 570 North Rossmore, across from the Wilshire Country Club and envision West, in her gravelly voice, beckoning visitors at the door to "come up and see me sometime." The star of *Everyday's a Holiday* (1938), *Klondike Annie* (1936), and *She Done Him Wrong* (1933), for most of her later life, lived in this cream-and-white satin-upholstered sanctuary. The shades, more often than not, were drawn.

Chapter One

Chapter Two

Hollywood
Hollywood Hills
West Hollywood

1. ROSANNA ARQUETTE/7704 Woodrow Wilson Dr.
2. HANK AZARIA • HELEN HUNT/6435 Bryn Mawr Dr.
3. KATHY BATES/2829 Westshire Dr.
4. HALLE BERRY/1368 Doheny Pl.
5. NICOLAS CAGE/4026 Woking Way
6. VONDIE CURTIS-HALL • KASI LEMMONS/8605 Appian Way
7. TIMOTHY DALTON/2707 Canyon Dr.
8. ARSENIO HALL/7740 Mulholland Dr.
9. HARRY HAMLIN/3007 Lake Glen Dr.
10. MADONNA/6342 Mulholland Hwy.
11. OZZIE & HARRIETT NELSON/1822 Comino Palermo
12. MATTHEW PERRY/7204 Chelan Way
13. JASON PRIESTLEY/2459 Park Oak Dr.
14. DAVID SCHWIMMER/1330 Londonderry Pl.
15. JERRY SEINFIELD/9444 Sierra Mar Pl.
16. ANDREW SHUE/2617 Outpost Dr.
17. SHARON STONE/7809 Torreyson Dr.
18. ORSON WELLES/8545 Franklin Ave.
19. LORETTA YOUNG/1308 North Flores St.

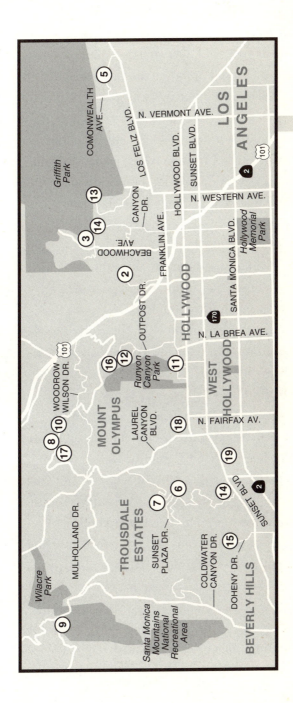

AT ABOUT THE SAME TIME
Los Angelenos were settling in West Adams and Hancock Park, an area known as Hollywood and also Hollywoodland was developing. Perched in the foothills above what was an unpaved Sunset Boulevard, Hollywood began to change with lightning speed due to the fledgling but instantly powerful movie business. Once again, economic factors would outweigh neighborhood values, and money transformed the once sleepy village of Hollywood into a city of diversity.

First, the small bungalows and mom-and-pop businesses were overshadowed by mansions built in the hills and along the major thoroughfares of Hollywood, Sunset, and Franklin. Pioneering filmmaker Mack Sennett created a mountaintop reverie. World-famous illusionist Harry Houdini settled into Laurel Canyon digs. Movie mogul Sam Goldwyn built an elegant home for his family off Franklin Avenue, which still stands today. Charlie Chaplin and the legendary Cecil B. DeMille ventured east to the area known as Los Feliz. The DeMille and Chaplin homes stand today next to one another at 2000 and 2010 DeMille Drive, a semiprivate area of elegant residences sharing a common drive.

In the hills above downtown Hollywood, dreamers built castles and pretended to be

European royalty. Madonna now lives in one of them—it's painted a deep terra-cotta color to give it the air of an Italian villa set in the chaparral hillside of what could be the Mediterranean coast of Italy. The Bernheimer family built their dream home fashioned in the style of a Japanese estate. Nothing like it has been seen before or since. Today the grand-scale residence and gardens are the Yamashiro Restaurant, perched on the hillside above Franklin, and open to the public.

From the 1920s through the 1950s, Hollywood was a glamorous place. Movie premieres sent beams of white skylight driven by powerful searchlights into the darkened sky on nearly daily occurrences. And the stars were always seen, looking their very best at all times, footprinting the cement at Grauman's Chinese Theater on Hollywood Boulevard (now Mann's Chinese Theater). The Hotel Roosevelt across the street hosted gala dinners in the evening, while by day the young and hopeful mingled with the newly rich and influential around its Olympic Pool bordered by gardens of enormous birds-of-paradise, banana trees, and queen palms.

The revolution of the 1960s in terms of American lifestyle and values began to erode the once elegant Hollywood. Members

Chapter Two

of the world's oldest profession replaced the likes of Marion Davies and Greta Garbo strolling the avenues. Nightclubs would shutter. Fancy boutiques became T-shirt shops. By 1970 all that remained of the grand old days was the popular bistro known as Musso & Frank on Hollywood Boulevard, which still operates, catering to the industry, as well as to the old Hollywood crowd.

Hollywood is now coming out of decline. The seedy elements have largely been replaced by a new urban look colored by young vision and energy. New stores and restaurants are popping up all over, and small neighborhoods are enjoying much stronger unity and everyday use by citizens who have chosen to live in areas such as Beachwood, Nichols, Laurel, Los Feliz, and Hollywood proper (resting between the famous Hollywood Bowl on North Highland and Cahuenga to the east). This movement is largely driven by young Hollywood. Many of these celebrities have chosen to make Hollywood home.

1 Rosanna Arquette

7704 Woodrow Wilson Drive
Los Angeles, CA 90046

THE SULTRY GENERATION X ACTRESS, WHOSE CREDITS include *The Wrong Man, Nowhere to Run, Sweet Revenge,* and *Ethan Frome,* lives at the top of Laurel Canyon. Her single-story stucco home with a pool, built in 1956, was purchased in 1992 for $790,000. The current market value is more than $1 million.

LOT SIZE: 9,683 SQ. FT.
HOME SIZE: 3, 047 SQ. FT.
ROOMS: 16, WITH 4 BEDROOMS, 4 BATHS

2 Hank Azaria / Helen Hunt

6435 Bryn Mawr Drive
Los Angeles, CA 90068

HANK AZARIA, CO-STAR OF *GODZILLA*, LIVES WITH Oscar®-winning actress Helen Hunt (*As Good As It Gets*) at 6435 Bryn Mawr Drive. The modern-style home, built in 1963, with a gravel roof and pool, is built on a small lot measuring 4,029 square feet, with a usable pad of 2,619 square feet. The two-bedroom, one and three-quarters bath residence was purchased by Azaria in 1992 for $390,000.

Chapter Two

Kathy Bates 3

2829 Westshire Drive
West Hollywood, CA 90068

> OSCAR®-WINNING ACTRESS KATHY BATES, CO-STAR OF *Titanic* in the role of Molly Brown, resides at 2829 Westshire Drive. An architecturally charming English-style home built in 1930, Bates has a wonderful garden view. The residence today is worth close to $1 million. The home was purchased in 1992 for a reported $750,000.

LOT SIZE: *8,505 SQ. FT.*
HOME SIZE: *3,421 SQ. FT.*
ROOMS: *12, WITH 3 BEDROOMS, AND 4 BATHS ON TWO STORIES*

Halle Berry 4

1368 Doheny Place
Los Angeles, CA 90069

> THIS BEAUTIFUL YOUNG ACTRESS TOOK THE NATION BY storm in the television miniseries *The Wedding*, and co-starred with Warren Beatty in *Bulworth*. This classically designed European villa with pool was built in 1989. It features high ceilings, expansive French windows, and marble, granite and hardwood floors, with custom detailing throughout the home. Its current market value is close to $2 million.

LOT SIZE: *14,349 SQ. FT*
HOME SIZE: *4,315 SQ. FT.*
ROOMS: *3 BEDROOMS, 4 BATHS*

5 Nicolas Cage

**4026 Woking Way
Los Angeles, CA 90027**

NICOLAS CAGE IS PERHAPS THE MOST SOUGHT-AFTER actor of his generation, with *Leaving Las Vegas*—for which he received a Best Actor Oscar®—among his many credits. He lives a private life in this contemporary home purchased in 1988 for $725,000. For a star whose salary is in the millions, the residence is a modest three-bedroom, four-bath, 2,390-square foot home.

6 Vondie Curtis-Hall Kasi Lemmons

**8605 Appian Way
Los Angeles, CA 90046**

THE TALENTED VONDIE CURTIS-HALL HAS RACKED UP AN impressive résumé, including such films as *Die Hard 2, Black Rain, Coming to America,* and more recently *Eve's Bayou, Romeo & Juliet,* and his own film *Gridlock'd,* which he directed.

Kasi Lemmons, with film credits including *Silence of the Lambs, Zooman,* and *'Til There Was You,* directed and wrote the screenplay for the critically acclaimed film *Eve's Bayou.*

This Mt. Olympus/Hollywood Hills retreat is the new home of Kasi Lemmons and Vondie Curtis-Hall. A reported sale price of $675,000 bought this view and pool residence for the young stars.

Chapter Two

Timothy Dalton 7

2707 Canyon Drive
Los Angeles, CA 90068

> ONE OF THE FEW LEADING MEN TO PLAY THE DASHING Secret Service agent James Bond, Welsh-born actor Timothy Dalton has credits ranging from *The Rocketeer* to *The Lion in Winter*. This modest Hollywood bungalow suits the actor's preference for a low-profile lifestyle.

HOME SIZE: 1,564 SQ. FT.
ROOMS: 7, WITH 1 BEDROOM, 2 BATHS
PURCHASE PRICE: $110,000

Arsenio Hall 8

7740 Mulholland Drive
Los Angeles, CA 90046

> THE FORMER LATE-NIGHT TELEVISION HOST, TURNED actor, lived on Mulholland Drive in the late 1980s when audiences were "woofing" it up with each new suit he wore. When he arrived home, Hall found a contem-porary residence with pool, spa, and view.

LOT SIZE: 12,197 SQ. FT.
HOME SIZE: 3,064 SQ. FT.
ROOMS: 10, WITH 2 BEDROOMS AND 3 BATHS
SOLD TO PRESENT OWNER: 1996
SALE AMOUNT: $730,000

9 Harry Hamlin

3007 Lake Glen Drive
Los Angeles, CA 90210

THIS HANDSOME LEADING MAN HAS ENJOYED A NEAR three-decade career on the large and small screen starring in such shows as *Master of the Game* on CBS, the NBC miniseries *Favorite Son*, and most notably the hit series *LA Law*, for which Hamlin was twice nominated for a Golden Globe. His film credits include *Making Love, King of the Mountain, Frogs for Snake,* and most recently *Bad Prospects*.

Hamlin owns this charming and substantial old residence built in 1939, featuring two-stories in 4,122 square feet, with a view and a pool.

LOT SIZE: *41,687* SQ. FT.
ROOMS: *15,* WITH *5* BEDROOMS AND *4* BATHS
ASSESSED VALUE: *$1,319,000*

HOLLYWOOD / HOLLYWOOD HILLS / WEST HOLLYWOOD

Chapter Two

Madonna 10

**6342 Mulholland Highway
Los Angeles, CA 90068**

THE BIGGEST MUSICAL AND FILM STAR OF HER GENERATION, Madonna, whose last film, *Evita*, was a critical success yet a box office disappointment, lives part time at this gated villa in the Hollywood Hills. Built in the 1920s, this residence was created in the grand castle–themed style of the day. Madonna was one of the performers who led the Hollywood migration back to the old neighborhoods when it was still considered pioneering to do so. She also owns other properties in Los Angeles, including a Westside home with a large, flat yard suitable for children.

ROOMS: 15, WITH 5 BEDROOMS AND 4 BATHS
ASSESSED VALUE: $1,319,800

Ozzie & Harriet Nelson 11

**1822 Camino Palermo
Los Angeles, CA 90046**

THE HANDSOME, OLD HOLLYWOOD FAMILY HOME WHERE Ozzie and Harriet raised David and Ricky Nelson, is a two-story, classic traditional with wood siding built in 1916. The home was sold to the present owner in 1993 for a reported $925,000. On a large, near half-acre lot, the residence features a pool and view.

LOT SIZE: 21,418 SQ. FT.
HOME SIZE: 5,214 SQ. FT.
ROOMS: 16, WITH 5 BEDROOMS AND 4 BATHS

12 Matthew Perry

7204 Chelan Way
Los Angeles, CA 90068

THIS SINGLE-STORY STUCCO HOME, CONTEMPORARY IN design, is the Hollywood home of *Friends* star Matthew Perry. There is a skinny-dipping pool with a view of the city. The present market value of the house is better than $650,000.

YEAR BUILT: 1959
LOT SIZE: 13,499 SQ. FT.
HOME SIZE: 1,902 SQ. FT.
ROOMS: 10, WITH 2 BEDROOMS, 3 BATHS
SALE DATE: MAY 1996
SALE AMOUNT: $590,000

13 Jason Priestley

2459 Park Oak Drive
Los Angeles, CA 90068

A YOUNG LEADING MAN OF THE SMALL SCREEN, JASON Priestley gained fame from his role in the popular television show *Beverly Hills, 90210*. Built in 1930, this two-story, Spanish-style abode has a pool and a view. Purchased in 1992 for $839,000, Priestley's home appreciates daily with the upswing in the market.

LOT SIZE: 12,449 SQ. FT.
HOME SIZE: 3,225 SQ. FT.
ROOMS: 11, WITH 4 BEDROOMS, 3 BATHS
ASSESSED VALUE: $858,600

Chapter Two

David Schwimmer 14

**1330 Londonderry Place
Los Angeles, CA 90068**

BUILT IN 1941, THIS TWO-STORY TRADITIONAL GEM WITH a beautiful pool and yard is the home of David Schwimmer of TV's *Friends*. The actor purchased the home in 1995 for a reported sale price of $750,000. The value of this home approaches $1 million.

LOT SIZE: **7,000** SQ. FT.
HOME SIZE: **3,193** SQ. FT.
ROOMS: **12**, WITH **4** BEDROOMS, **3** BATHS

Jerry Seinfeld 15

**9444 Sierra Mar Place
Los Angeles, CA**

THE "FUNNIEST GUY IN AMERICA" LIVES IN A PRETTY serious contemporary home with jetliner views of the entire Los Angeles basin. Jerry Seinfeld may have more time to enjoy his enormous modern home, now that this television series has finished a near decade-long run.

Situated on a winding drive called Sierra Mar Place, the Seinfeld pad is a long, low 1960s contemporary that has been totally renovated to 1990s standards. The soft gray-and-white-trimmed stucco residence with walls of floor-to-ceiling tinted glass contains twenty rooms and garage space for more than ten cars.

Purchased in 1992 for a reported $2,800,000, the Seinfeld home has 5,913 square feet and can be seen from lower Sierra Mar Place, behind the home. From the front all one will see are garage doors and a gate. A speeding black Porsche winding up the hills is likely to belong to the owner. Be careful and pull over—Jerry is one fast driver.

HOME SIZE: 5,913 SQ. FT.
ROOMS: 20, WITH 4 BEDROOMS AND 4 BATHS
SALE PRICE: $2,800,000
SALE DATE: 1992

16 Andrew Shue

2617 Outpost Drive
Los Angeles, CA 90068

OUTPOST ESTATES, A VERY OLD, ELEGANT, AND EXCLUSIVE section of Hollywood north of Franklin Avenue and west of La Brea Avenue, is still home to many stars. One of its younger residents, handsome actor Andrew Shue, former star of Aaron Spelling's hit show *Melrose Place*, lives here with wife Jennifer.

The two-story traditional home sits on a near half-acre lot. Built in 1952, the home became part of the Andrew and Jennifer Shue Trust in 1995. The price? $582,000 TV-earned dollars.

LOT SIZE: 20,970 SQ. FT.
HOUSE SIZE: 1,588 SQ. FT.
ROOMS: 9, WITH 3 BEDROOMS, 3 BATHS
ASSESSED VALUE: $593,600

Chapter Two

Sharon Stone 17

7809 Torreyson Drive
Los Angeles, CA 90046

NOW REGISTERED AS OWNED BY THE MILLICENT CRAVEN Trust, this Hollywood residence was home to screen star Sharon Stone during the 1980s. The residence was built in 1955.

LOT SIZE: 15,678 SQ. FT.
HOME SIZE: 1,966 SQ. FT.
ROOMS: 7, WITH 2 BEDROOMS AND 1 BATH
ASSESSED VALUE: $569,425
SALE AMOUNT: $1,035,000

Orson Welles 18

8545 Franklin Avenue
Los Angeles, CA 90069

CONSIDERED BY MANY TO BE THE FINEST TWENTIETH-century director, actor, and writer in the medium of film, Orson Welles died a troubled man in 1985. Welles, who made *Citizen Kane* and acted in *Prince of Foxes,* lived at this home for a time when he was coming up the Hollywood ranks. The residence has a remodeled (1975) kitchen. Built in 1933, it sits on a standard lot in West Hollywood in an area that has changed and evolved much over the years. The present market value is more than $400,000.

LOT SIZE: 6,970 SQ. FT.
HOME SIZE: 2,400 SQ. FT.
ROOMS: 11, WITH 3 BEDROOMS AND 3 BATHS

19 Loretta Young

1308 North Flores Street
Los Angeles, CA 90068

BORN IN SALT LAKE CITY, UTAH, AS GRETCHEN MICHAELA Young, this woman became one of the great beauties of the silver screen. Starring in such films as *The Farmer's Daughter* (1947), for which she won an Academy Award®, and *The Story of Alexander Graham Bell* (1939), Young lived all over L.A. first with her mother and sisters, then with husbands Grant Withers and Thomas Lewis. Recently widowed from third husband Jean Louis, Young lives in the Deepwell Ranch section of Palm Springs. At one time in her early career, she lived in West Hollywood at 1308 North Flores Street. Young's last L.A. address was a John Wolf–designed French Regency manor house in Beverly Hills at the corner of Benedict Canyon and Ambassador Drive. The property with two bedrooms, a pool, and enough closet space for a "star," sold several years ago for under $1 million.

Chapter Three

Beverly Hills

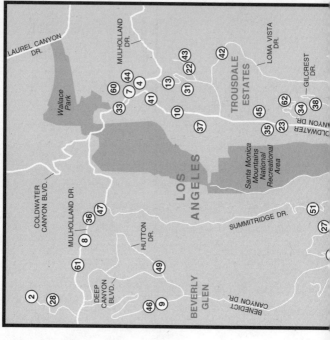

1. JULIE ANDREWS/135 Copley Pl.
2. TOM ARNOLD/14046 Aubrey Rd.
3. LUCILLE BALL • DESI ARNAZ
   1000 N. Roxbury Dr.
4. WARREN BEATTY/13671 Mulholland Dr.
5. LAURALEE BELL/425 N. Maple Dr.
6. ERNEST BORGNINE/1720 Chevy Chase Dr.
7. MARLON BRANDO/12900 Mulholland Dr.
8. MICHAEL CAINE/2069 Coldwater Cyn. Dr.
9. DIAHANN CARROLL/2660 Benedict Cyn.
10. SHAUN CASSIDY/13255 Mulholland Dr.
11. CYD CHARISSE • TONY MARTIN
    1114 Calle Vista Dr.
12. AL CHECCHI • SIDNEY POITIER
    1007 Cove Way
13. JOAN COLLINS/2220 Bowmont Dr.
14. PHIL COLLINS/9401 Sunset Blvd.
15. ROBERT CUMMINGS/100 Laurel Way
16. MARION DAVIES/1700 Lexington.

17. MARVIN DAVIS • KENNY ROGERS
1130 Schuyler Rd.
18. DORIS DAY/713 N. Crescent Dr.
19. NEIL DIAMOND/904 Glen Way
20. KIRK DOUGLAS/805 N. Rexford Dr.
21. FAYE DUNAWAY/714 Palm Dr.
22. LINDA EVANS/9115 Hazen Dr.
23. CARRIE FISHER/1700 Coldwater Cyn. Dr.
24. ELLA FITZGERALD/718 N. Sierra Dr.
25. GLENN FORD/911 Oxford Way
26. DAVID GEFFEN • JACK WARNER
1801 Angelo Dr.
27. CARY GRANT/9966 Beverly Grove Dr.
28. WAYNE GRETZKY/14135 Beresford Rd.
29. GEORGE HAMILTON/1100 Carolyn Way
30. JEAN HARLOW/512 N. Palm Dr.
31. WOODY HARRELSON/2387 Kimridge Rd.
32. REX HARRISON/1106 San Ysidro Dr.
33. CHARLTON HESTON/2859 Coldwater Cyn. Dr.
34. ROCK HUDSON/9402 Beverly Crest Dr.
35. DON JOHNSON/9555 Heather Rd.
36. MAGIC JOHNSON/13100 Mulholland Dr.
37. DIANE LADD/2241 Betty Lane
38. ESTHER WILLIAMS LAMAS/
9377 Readcrest Dr.
39. STEVE LAWRENCE & EYDIE GORME
820 Greenway Dr.
40. JAY LENO/1151 & 1149 Tower Rd.
41. ANN-MARGRET/2727 Coldwater Cyn. Dr.
42. DEAN MARTIN/2002 Loma Vista Dr.
43. STEVE MARTIN/9136 Calle Juella
44. ED McMAHON/12000 Crest Court
45. DUDLEY MOORE • SUSAN ANTON
1853 Noel Pl.
46. EDDIE MURPHY/2727 Benedict Cyn.
47. JACK NICHOLSON/12850 Mulholland Dr.
48. JACK PALANCE/1006 Hartford Way
49. STEFANIE POWERS/2661 Hutton Dr.

50. ELVIS PRESLEY/144 Monovale Dr.
51. PRISCILLA PRESLEY/1167 Summit Dr.
52. CARL REINER/714 N. Rodeo Dr.
53. DEBBIE REYNOLDS/813 Greenway Dr.
54. SMOKEY ROBINSON/631 N. Oakhurst Dr.
55. GEORGE SEGAL/841 Greenway Dr.
56. DINAH SHORE/916 Oxford Dr.
57. FRANK SINATRA/915 N. Foothill Rd.
58. TOM SNYDER/1225 Beverly Estates Terr.
59. JIMMY STEWART/918 N. Roxbury
60. DAMON WAYANS/12089 Summit Circle
61. BRUCE WILLIS • DEMI MOORE
13511 Mulholland Dr.
62. JAMES WOODS/1612 Gilcrest Dr.
63. PIA ZADORA
DOUGLAS FAIRBANKS & MARY
PICKFORD/1143 Summit Dr.

31

TO THE RICH AND FAMOUS OF THE entertainment world, Beverly Hills is mecca. Home to more celebrities than any other neighborhood on the planet, this former bean ranch in the sage-covered foothills of the Santa Monica Mountains was originally transformed by developers in search of the real estate dollar, and propelled by the migration of stars that followed the building of Douglas Fairbanks and Mary Pickford's Pickfair.

Life was good. The weather was better here and when the career was on a roll and money was no object, grand homes and estates began to appear. Right up until the crash of 1929, and in some cases during and beyond the stock market failure, movie money was building, building, building. The nickels kept coming in to the movie world, despite the lack of food in America. There was good reason to go to a movie and forget.

A cornerstone of Beverly Hills life and society was the then stand-alone Beverly Hills Hotel at the corner of Sunset Boulevard and Crescent Drive. Today, owned by the Sultan of Brunei, this pink palace of glitz remains a focal point of the community's social life. However, all things do change, and the glory days of movie stars lounging by the pool and sipping champagne in the Polo Lounge have largely been replaced by movie deal makers and TV and record executives schmoozing in the hopes of making a killing.

Some of the great names of the golden era, such as Tony Curtis, can still be seen, a beautiful blonde on his arm, enjoying a drink in the Polo Lounge. Often, everyone in the room is looking at everyone else to see who is who. Some things never change, just the faces, the clothes, and the food, which is still excellent and served with great style.

Beverly Hills 90210 is really made up of many neighborhoods. Each is distinctive. Grand estates can be found on Sunset Boulevard and north of the grand thoroughfare. In the hills behind the Beverly Hills Hotel, one will find some of the most amazing residential architecture in the nation. And just about every house has a story. In fact, most probably have more than one story since movie stars often move. And they move frequently, so many homes bear multiple pedigrees.

The flats of Beverly Hills, which are simply the flat residential streets laid out in a grid between Sunset to the north, Santa Monica to the south, Doheny to the east, and Whittier to the west, are row after row of exceptionally handsome homes, most all

Chapter Three

visible from the street. Nearly every one of them was once the residence of someone you might have worshiped on film, on televi-sion, or in the recording industry. Those that have not been inhabited by stars were largely the homes of industry executives, including major directors, producers, and writers. The Hollywood crowd attracts Los Angeles's most successful among the business, sports, and medical communities as well.

Another of the distinct Beverly Hills neighborhoods is known as the Post Office. Why? Because the area is actually not in Beverly Hills, it's part of Los Angeles. However, it is served by the Beverly Hills Post Office because at one time it was the only one in proximity. Residents of the Beverly Hills Post Office region enjoy the coveted 90210 zip code made world famous by the Aaron Spelling television drama of the same name. They live in the uppermost canyons adjacent to Beverly Hills proper, and in developments and estate sites off of the world-renowned Mulholland Drive, which divides Los Angeles and the San Fernando Valley.

Beverly Hills is home to some of the city's great estates, including the Doheny Mansion, located of course on Doheny Road and now used by the Academy of Motion Picture

Arts and Sciences and the City of Beverly Hills. Silent screen pioneer Harold Lloyd created Greenacres on twenty-some acres of canyon at a cost of several million dollars. The estate, on Greenacres Drive off of Benedict Canyon, passed through the Lloyd family to several owners, including filmmaker Ted Field. It is now the home of the Ron Berkel family, who reportedly paid in excess of $30 million for the estate in the early 1990s. Berkel, a supermarket magnate, is a close friend of President Bill Clinton, and the president often stays at Greenacres when in Los Angeles.

Pickfair, the home that started it all, is now the residence of Pia Zadora, the singer-actress and estranged wife of billionaire and international businessman Meshulam Riklis. Prior to their marital difficulties, Riklis bought the mansion and transformed the old hunting lodge into a European villa, reportedly spending more than $20 million in its restoration, then filling it with countless millions in fine art. Another of the great estates is known as The Knoll, just off Doheny Road at Schuyler Road. The Knoll, which cannot be seen from the street (only the massive gates are visible) is presently the residence of movie mogul and oil billionaire Marvin Davis, who once presided over 20th Century Fox. Singer Kenny Rogers and his family lived at The Knoll

Chapter Three

prior to the Davis ownership. Rogers sold The Knoll to Davis in the 1980s for what was then the highest price paid for residential real estate in the world: a record $23 million.

The 1980s was the beginning of the mind-blowing multiple-digit celebrity land rush. Producer and entrepreneur David Geffen would make headlines in the early 1990s purchasing the Jack Warner estate and paying in excess of $40 million for the furnished property from the Warner heirs. Mouths flapped over the record price, which in true Geffen form turned out to be a value, considering the fact that the antique furniture filling the estate was all of collector quality, bringing in millions at auction.

From the 1930s through well into the 1980s, Beverly Hills was the unofficial home to the stars. The 1990s have been a decade of change in Beverly Hills, one that has transformed this fancy village of movie stars and wealthy American families into a truly international city of diverse culture and changing values. You'll see it all here—the estates, the restaurants, the shops including Rodeo Drive, in this land of plenty that was made by Hollywood.

1 Julie Andrews

135 Copley Place
Beverly Hills, CA 90210

VICTOR, VICTORIA AND THE SOUND OF MUSIC STAR Julie Andrews and her husband, director Blake Edwards, have lived in numerous residences from Malibu to Brentwood to Beverly Hills. This elegant, twenty-room mansion, on Copley Place just off Sunset Boulevard, is one of the most notable. It is listed in architectural guides of the city as the Holmes House. Built in 1933 and designed by Gordon B. Kaufman, it is described as a "beautiful and carefully proportioned Spanish-style dwelling, accompanied by terraces, pools, and summer house." Estimated property value for the eight-bedroom, seven-bath property Andrews once called home is estimated at more than $5 million.

LOT SIZE: 43,560 SQ. FT.
HOME SIZE: 9,517 SQ. FT.

2 Tom Arnold

14046 Aubrey Road
Beverly Hills, CA 90210

TOM ARNOLD, COMEDIC STAR AND FORMER HUSBAND OF Roseanne, and his new wife recently closed escrow on this modern mansion in the gated community of Mulholland Estates. This $2.3 million plus home has nearly 6,800 square feet in two stories with five bedrooms, six and one-half baths, maid's quarters, pool, and a six-car garage. Built in 1990 in Spanish Gothic style, this villa originally belonged to pop star Paula Abdul.

Lucille Ball 3
Desi Arnaz

1000 North Roxbury Drive
Beverly Hills, CA 90210

> Recently remodeled and redesigned by its new owner, 1000 North Roxbury was the handsome, traditional East Coast colonial-style residence of world-famous comedian Lucille Ball and her bandleader husband, Desi Arnaz, for many years. After their divorce, Ball remarried and remained in the Roxbury residence until her death.

Warren Beatty 4

13671 Mulholland Drive
Beverly Hills, CA 90210

> Purchased in 1974 for $193,000, 13671 Mulholland Drive has been home to actor/director Warren Beatty, star of *Bulworth* (1998), *Heaven Can Wait* (1978), *Reds* (1981), and *Shampoo* (1975). Built in 1938, the remodeled twenty-room residence with 9,401 square feet on a 3.4-acre site includes five bedrooms and eight baths. His most recent tax assessment placed the value of the property at $925,043, and Beatty pays taxes of $10,204.01 per year. The real market value is considerably higher, perhaps well over $5 million.

5 Lauralee Bell

425 North Maple Drive
Beverly Hills, CA 90210

VOTED FAVORITE SOAP OPERA ACTRESS IN 1989 BY *Teen Magazine*, Lauralee Bell, born December 22, 1968, in Chicago, Illinois, is the daughter of soap opera creators William and Lee Phillip Bell. Lauralee appeared on her parents' show *The Young and the Restless* from 1986 until 1996. The Bell family is one of the wealthiest and most influential partnerships in daytime television. Lauralee's brother, Bradley, is the executive producer of another Bell show, *The Bold and the Beautiful*.

An elegant new French-chateau condo that has been home to stars such as Rod Stewart and Richard Chamberlain is the residence of this rising television star. The building, with a New York feel and very formal apartments, sits on the northwest corner of Beverly Boulevard and Maple Drive. Bell also owns property in Malibu (see Chapter Nine).

HOME SIZE: 3,109 SQ. FT.
ROOMS: 4 BEDROOMS, 6 BATHS
PURCHASED BY BELL: 1991
PURCHASE PRICE: $1,300,000

Chapter Three

Ernest Borgnine 6

1720 Chevy Chase Drive
Beverly Hills, CA 90210

TODAY *MCHALE'S NAVY* STAR ERNEST BORGNINE AND his wife, cosmetics entrepreneur Tova, share an active Beverly Hills life. However, this swank home at 1720 Chevy Chase Drive, off Benedict Canyon, once had the Borgnine pedigree when he was making such classic movies as *The Dirty Dozen* (1967), *Marty* (1955) (for which Borgnine won and Oscar®), and *From Here To Eternity* (1953).

The Borgnines resided in this nineteen-room Spanish mansion with three bedrooms, six baths, and pool in the 1970s and 1980s.

YEAR BUILT: 1926
LOT SIZE: 15,198 SQ. FT.
HOME SIZE: 4,908 SQ. FT.

Marlon Brando 7

12900 Mulholland Drive
Beverly Hills, CA 90210

BEST KNOWN FOR HIS ROLES AS THE BROODING HUSBAND in Tennessee Williams's *A Streetcar Named Desire,* and as Don Corleone in *The Godfather,* Marlon Brando lives in a semi-reclusive estate at 12900 Mulholland Drive. Built in 1954, the twelve-room residence with pool, designed in contemporary style, has three bedrooms, four baths, and a sumptuous view. The assessed value of the property is $239,133, and the estimated market value today is $1 million plus.

8 Michael Caine
2069 Coldwater Canyon Drive
Beverly Hills, CA 90210

A WONDERFUL OLD RESIDENCE, BUILT IN 1939 WITH great traditional colonial style, thirteen rooms, and a pool, is the residence of acclaimed English actor Michael Caine, whose heavy-lidded charm and intelligence made him the star of *Alfie* and *Educating Rita*. The two-story home was previously owned by James Cagney.

LOT SIZE: **4.35 ACRES**
HOME SIZE: **3,578 SQ. FT.**
PURCHASED BY CAINE IN: **1987**
PURCHASE PRICE: **$1,800,000**

9 Diahann Carroll
2660 Benedict Canyon
Beverly Hills, CA 90210

THE BEAUTIFUL DIAHANN CARROLL, ACTRESS (*CLAUDINE*, 1974, and *Porgy and Bess*, 1959), and singer, with and without husband Vic Damone, has lived in a number of Beverly Hills homes, including 2660 Benedict Canyon. She and Damone lived high atop Beverly Hills in a very chic European villa in Trousdale Estates with a city view and pool on the edge of the mountainside. Both homes have been sold.

Chapter Three

Shaun Cassidy 10
13255 Mulholland Drive
Beverly Hills, CA 90210

> This former teen television and singing idol, star of *The Hardy Boys*, has become a serious stage and musical theater performer. Cassidy lived in this single-family home in the 1980s. Built in 1949, on a large lot with a view and a pool, this one-story house consists of twelve rooms, including four bedrooms and four baths.

Lot Size: 27,510 sq. ft.
Home Size: 3,165 sq. ft.

Cyd Charisse 11
Tony Martin
1114 Calle Vista Drive
Beverly Hills, CA 90210

> Trousdale, a hillside enclave built by developer Paul Trousdale in the 1960s and 1970s, was home to dancer Cyd Charisse (*Singin' in the Rain* and *The Band Wagon*) and her husband, Tony Martin. This neighborhood, in the hills above Sunset Boulevard, boasts incredible views.

Lot Size: 43,996 sq. ft.
Home Size: 3,760 sq. ft.
Rooms: 15, with 3 bedrooms and 5 baths
Sale Date: 1981
Sale Amount: $1,153,500

12 Al Checchi
(current owner)
Sidney Poitier
(previous owner)

1007 Cove Way
Beverly Hills, CA 90210

THE PRESENT OWNER, AL CHECCHI, IS A SELF-MADE businessman who ran for Governor of California, but won't be living in the Governor's Mansion in Sacramento. Built in 1927, this estate features twenty-six rooms including ten bedrooms and seven baths in 8,400 square feet. Its market value is more than $5 million. The European-styled mansion was once the home of the talented Sidney Poitier, star of such films as *Guess Who's Coming to Dinner, To Sir With Love, A Raisin in the Sun,* and most recently *The Jackal.*

13 Joan Collins

2220 Bowmont Drive
Beverly Hills, CA 90210

ONCE THE HOME OF TELEVISION STAR AND AUTHOR JOAN Collins, this traditional home, built in 1936, was headquarters for Collins's own "Dynasty." Title records show the British-born actress sold the home to the present owner in 1996 for a reported $775,500.

LOT SIZE: **14,228** *SQ. FT.*
HOME SIZE: **4,888** *SQ. FT.*
ROOMS: **13,** *WITH* **4** *BEDROOMS AND* **5** *BATHS*

Chapter Three

Phil Collins 14

9401 Sunset Boulevard
Beverly Hills, CA 90210

BRITISH ROCKER PHIL COLLINS PURCHASED A LEGENDARY, old-world English estate at the northwest corner of Sunset Boulevard and Hillcrest Drive in the early 1990s for a reported $8 million. The manor needed total restoration, so Collins, his wife, and design team dug in, spending millions more. The project is yet to be fully completed. Collins has separated from his wife in the process.

Robert Cummings 15

1060 Laurel Way
Beverly Hills, CA 90210

BUILT IN 1949 FOR HANDSOME STAR ROBERT CUMMINGS, who appeared in *Kings Row* (1942), *The Devil and Miss Jones* (1941), and *Spring Parade* (1940), today's market value of this two-story contemporary-style home with a pool exceeds $3.5 million.

LOT SIZE: **36,586** SQ. FT.
HOME SIZE: **7,593** SQ. FT.
ROOMS: **22**, WITH **7** BEDROOMS AND **7** BATHS

16 Marion Davies

1700 Lexington Road
Beverly Hills, CA 90210

ONE OF THE GRAND OLD ESTATES, 1700 LEXINGTON ROAD in the 1920s and 1930s was owned by Marion Davies, film siren and paramour of communications star William Randolph Hearst. The handsome English brick residence, built in 1923, painted white today, sits on a knoll of prime real estate on more than one acre of land. Four bedrooms and four baths with a pool, the estate is worth in excess of $4 million.

LOT SIZE: 56,070 SQ. FT.
HOME SIZE: 6,024 SQ. FT.

17 Marvin Davis
(current owner)
Kenny Rogers
(previous owner)

1130 Schuyler Road
Beverly Hills, CA 90210

THE KNOLL IS AN ESTATE OF INTERNATIONAL REPUTATION. It belongs to Marvin and Barbara Davis, whose oil-, real estate-, and movie-rich family operates on a worldwide level. Built in 1955 in the French International style, this forty-two–room mansion has 25,437 square feet of living space on over ten acres. When the Davis family purchased the property from country singer Kenny Rogers for a reported $20 million-plus figure, the purchase was the largest single-family–residence transaction in the world.

Chapter Three

Doris Day 18

713 North Crescent Drive
Beverly Hills, CA 90210

SHE LIT UP THE SILVER SCREEN FOR DECADES. PERHAPS best known for her romantic comedies of the 1950s and 1960s such as *Pillow Talk* with Rock Hudson and *The Pajama Game*, beautiful Doris Day owned 713 North Crescent Drive until recently putting the property on the market. The contemporary home, which had been added on to and remodeled over the years, served in later years as a rental property for Day.

HOME SIZE: 4,309 SQ. FT.
ROOMS: 13, WITH 3 BEDROOMS AND 4 BATHS

Neil Diamond 19

904 Glen Way
Beverly Hills, CA 90210

BALLADEER NEIL DIAMOND, WHOSE VOICE AND STYLE IS indelibly implanted in his interpretations of "Cracklin' Rosie," and "Song Sung Blue," lives in a massive contemporary home at 904 Glen Way behind the Beverly Hills Hotel. Built in 1979, the estate houses Diamond's art collection and contains eight bedrooms, eleven baths, and a pool.

LOT SIZE: 2 ACRES
HOME SIZE: 10,706 SQ. FT.
ASSESSED VALUE: $4,600,000

20 Kirk Douglas

805 North Rexford Drive
Beverly Hills, CA 90210

SPARTACUS LEADING MAN KIRK DOUGLAS AND HIS WIFE, Anne, enjoy life at the elegantly remodeled 805 North Rexford Drive. The totally rebuilt Mediterranean-style residence is more than double its original size. Originally, the eleven-room house had three bedrooms and four baths in just 3,098 square feet. Purchased by the Douglases in 1976, the current market value on this newly rebuilt home would exceed $4 million.

21 Faye Dunaway

714 North Palm Drive
Beverly Hills, CA 90210

IT'S BEEN MORE THAN A DECADE SINCE INTERNATIONAL film star and Academy Award®-winning star of *Network* and *Chinatown*, Faye Dunaway, resided in the flats of Beverly Hills. When she was in residence, her home of choice was 714 North Palm Drive. This lovely traditional home was totally redone in 1987.

LOT SIZE: 24,300 SQ. FT.
HOME SIZE: 9,960 SQ. FT.
ROOMS: 18, INCLUDING 5 BEDROOMS AND 9 BATHS
ASSESSED VALUE: $2,403,00

BEVERLY HILLS

Chapter Three 47

Linda Evans 22

9115 Hazen Drive
Beverly Hills, CA 90210

TV's LEADING LADY, LINDA EVANS, THE SEXY BLOND star of the hit 1980s drama *Dynasty*, now an exercise and fitness guru, lives in this cozy English-style country home in verdant Coldwater Canyon off Cherokee Road on Hazen Drive. The master bedroom features a fireplace, sauna, and steam room with spa. A grand living room, den with bar, private pool, and two maid's rooms complement the Evans home. The gated property was built in 1937 and also has four family bedrooms and six baths. The current market value of the property is estimated at $1,650,000, the asking price at which Evans listed her home for sale. By the way, if you were in the market for a celebrity rental, this could be yours for around $8,500 per month.

LOT SIZE: *19,140* SQ. FT.
HOME SIZE: *3,904* SQ. FT.

23 Carrie Fisher

1700 Coldwater Canyon Drive
Beverly Hills, CA 90210

DEBBIE REYNOLDS AND EDDIE FISHER'S LITTLE GIRL, Carrie, has done quite well for herself as a writer and actor. Her first leading role was in *Shampoo* (1975), playing a young seductress to leading man Warren Beatty. Carrie Fisher went on to star as Princess Leia in the *Star Wars* trilogy. Following recovery from drug and alcohol dependency, Fisher emerged to co-star in such films as *When Harry Met Sally* (1989) and *Soapdish* (1991). The publication of her autobiographical novel *Postcards From the Edge* attracted tremendous attention, both from an admiring public and from within the industry. Director Mike Nichols hired Fisher to script her book for the 1990 film by the same name. She has since written a number of other scripts and additional novels including *Delusions of Grandma*.

Purchased by Fisher in 1993 at a reported sale amount of $3,745,592, this wonderful old home with a pool was built in 1933.

LOT SIZE: 3 ACRES
HOME SIZE: 4,210 SQ. FT.
ROOMS: 10, WITH 4 BEDROOMS AND 4 BATHS

Chapter Three

Ella Fitzgerald 24

718 North Sierra Drive
Beverly Hills, CA 90210

> THE LEGENDARY JAZZ SINGER ELLA FITZGERALD CALLED 718 North Sierra Drive in Beverly Hills flats her home. Built in 1951, the traditional residence contains twelve rooms, including five bedrooms, six baths, and a pool. Fitzgerald purchased this home in 1975 for $262,000, and the property was sold in 1994 to a new owner for $1,500,000.

*LOT SIZE: **26,260** SQ. FT.*
*HOME SIZE: **5,593** SQ. FT.*

Glenn Ford 25

911 Oxford Way
Beverly Hills, CA 90210

> DURING THE HOLLYWOOD GOLDEN ERA, THIS LEADING man whose credits included *The Man From Alamo* (1953), *Gilda* (1946), and *A Stolen Life* (1946), owned a contemporary home with a pool behind the Beverly Hills Hotel. Sitting on seven acres of valuable land, the house, built in 1962, features three bedrooms and six baths. Given the land and the possible development opportunity, the Glenn Ford Living Trust, which owns this parcel, could be sitting on a $20 million-plus real estate investment.

*HOME SIZE: **8, 552** SQ. FT.*

26 David Geffen
(current owner)
Jack Warner
(previous owner)

1801 Angelo Drive
Beverly Hills, CA 90210

A MAJOR PLAYER IN THE ENTERTAINMENT INDUSTRY, David Geffen turned his record empire into movies, television, studio ownership, and much more, landing on top of the *Forbes* 400 list of wealthiest Americans. Fittingly, several years ago Geffen purchased the ultimate piece of Los Angeles residential real estate: the Jack Warner (of Warner Bros. fame) estate. Built in 1937, 1801 Angelo Drive has thirty rooms, including eight bedrooms and nine baths. Rumored to have been purchased fully furnished for near $40 million, the Greek Revival mansion underwent total renovation at the hands of its new owner.

LOT SIZE: 9.38 ACRES
HOME SIZE: 13,612 SQ. FT.

BEVERLY HILLS

Chapter Three

Cary Grant 27

**9966 Beverly Grove Drive
Beverly Hills, CA 90210**

CARY GRANT, THE HANDSOME LEADING MAN WHO defined sophisticated romantic comedy for audiences worldwide, starred in *North by Northwest* (1959), *To Catch a Thief* (1955), and *The Philadelphia Story* (1940). Married numerous times, his wives included heiress Barbara Hutton (the pair was referred to as "Cash and Cary") and actress Dyan Cannon, with whom he had his only child, Jennifer.

During his lifetime and long career, Grant lived in many places from modest to grand. This estate, with its 7,477 square foot home, was his final residence with wife Barbara Harris (who still resides there).

Wayne Gretzky 28

**14135 Beresford Road
Beverly Hills, CA 90210**

HOCKEY HAS TAKEN AMERICA BY STORM. ONE OF TODAY'S biggest names in the sport is Canadian-born Wayne Gretzky who, besides having a passion for hockey, happens to love houses and cars as well.

Gretzky and his family presently live in Mulholland Estates, a gate-guarded enclave of fashionable new mansions set in the hills on the San Fernando Valley side of Mulholland Drive, just east of Beverly Glen.

Their white colonial two-story estate, built in 1989, at 14135 Beresford Road, behind the Mulholland Estates gate, has five bedrooms, six baths, and a major San Fernando Valley view.

Home Size: 6,896 sq. ft.
Purchased by Gretsky in: 1991
Purchase Price: $3,450,000

29 George Hamilton

1100 Carolyn Way
Beverly Hills, CA 90210

For many years, the actor who starred in *Zorro: The Gay Blade* (1981) and *Where the Boys Are* (1960) lived until the 1990s in this Beverly Hills mansion, once the home of legendary silent screen pioneer Charlie Chaplin. Built in 1916, the three-story formal Mediterranean-influenced residence has thirty-nine rooms, including eight bedrooms, twelve baths, and a pool. Hamilton sold the house in 1992 to the present owner at a price reportedly exceeding $6 million.

Lot Size: 1 acre
Home Size: 14,765 sq. ft.

Chapter Three

Jean Harlow 30

512 North Palm Drive
Beverly Hills, Ca 90210

Jean Harlow was one of the biggest stars of the 1930s. Born in Kansas City, Missouri, March 3, 1911, the blond actress, who starred in *Bombshell* (1933), *Dinner at Eight* (1933), and *Public Enemy* (1931), to name a few, challenged Marlene Dietrich as the anointed sexiest screen siren. In her short lifetime, Harlow lived all over town. One of her best addresses was 512 North Palm Drive in Beverly Hills. At the time Harlow lived here, the charming Spanish bungalow built in 1928 was near new. It was not grand by standards then and now, but it was certainly a lovely home of substance.

Lot Size: 11,709 sq. ft.
Home Size: 4,426 sq. ft.
Rooms: 15, with 5 bedrooms and 5 baths
Assessed value today: $1,192,160

Woody Harrelson 31

2387 Kimridge Road
Beverly Hills, CA 90210

Bad boy Woody Harrelson, star of *Natural Born Killers, Money Train,* and *The People v. Larry Flynt,* lives quite stylishly in a one-story contemporary residence built in 1952 with a pool and a commanding hillside view. The three-bedroom, four-bath home sits on a more than half-acre lot. Harrelson purchased his hillside retreat in 1989 at a reported sale price of $1,800,000.

32 Rex Harrison

1106 San Ysidro Drive
Beverly Hills, CA 90210

ACADEMY AWARD® WINNER AND THE DAPPER STAR OF *My Fair Lady,* the late Rex Harrison lived—during the 1970s—in this contemporary California home built in 1959. A stucco exterior and a gravel roof are the trademarks of this one-story house with sixteen rooms, including four bedrooms and a pool, set in a canyon above Beverly Hills.

LOT SIZE: 16,980 SQ. FT.
HOME SIZE: 4,708 SQ. FT.

33 Charlton Heston

2859 Coldwater Canyon Drive
Beverly Hills, CA 90210

BORN CHARLES CARTER ON OCTOBER 4, 1923, CHARLTON Heston is best known for his role as Moses in Cecil B. DeMille's epic *The Ten Commandments* (1956). Other film credits include *The Agony and the Ecstasy* (1965), *El Cid* (1961), and *Ben Hur* (1959), for which he won the Best Actor Oscar®.

The politically conservative, outspoken activist currently lives with his wife in a private fashion despite his well-publicized forays into social issues.

YEAR BUILT: 1959
HOME SIZE: 5,083 SQ. FT.

Chapter Three

Rock Hudson 34

9402 Beverly Crest Drive
Beverly Hills, CA 90210

ROY SCHERER, THE HANDSOME, RAVEN-HAIRED MID-western boy from Winnetka, Illinois, turned Hollywood upside down after his small role in *Fighter Squadron* (1948). Hudson went on to star in such films as *Send Me No Flowers* (1964), *Magnificent Obsession*, and *Giant* (1956).

In the days when Hudson was a Universal Studios contract player, he lived at 9402 Beverly Crest Drive.

YEAR BUILT: 1942
HOME SIZE: 8,086 SQ. FT.
ROOMS: 7 BEDROOMS, 8 BATHS

Don Johnson 35

9555 Heather Road
Beverly Hills, CA 90210

BARBRA STREISAND'S FORMER BOYFRIEND, MELANIE Griffith's former husband, and the star of the hit TV series *Nash Bridges* is none other than Heather Road resident Don Johnson.

HOME SIZE: 5,847 SQ. FT.
ROOMS: 22, WITH 5 BEDROOMS AND 6 BATHS
TAXES: $23,791.98 PER YEAR
ASSESSED VALUE: $2,209,000

36 Earvin "Magic" Johnson Jr.

13100 Mulholland Drive
Beverly Hills, CA 90210

THIS LARGE CONTEMPORARY HOME ON A HILL HOUSED the superstar of basketball during his playing career with the Lakers. Magic sold the house in the late 1980s and moved with his wife, Cookie, to a massive Mediterranean-style estate in the exclusive enclave known as Beverly Park, not far from his old residence.

Beverly Park is a gated, guarded community perched high atop the hills of Beverly, accessible via San Ysidro Drive on the city side and Mulholland Drive on the Valley side. Beverly Park, a development of estates that sit on pads of one acre or more, carry price tags in excess of $5 million, with many exceeding $10 million. Residents of Beverly Park include Disney chairman Michael Eisner, *Power Rangers* promoter Haim Saban, and international financier Meshulam Riklis.

The Johnsons listed their present residence in Beverly Park for sale in the summer of 1998. The estate, which features a gym (of course), tennis court, pool, media center, and game room that includes everything available to humankind, went on the market for just under $8 million. The residence has approx-imately 14,000 square feet, with exceptionally tall ceilings and doors.

If you drive up San Ysidro to the very top of the hill, you will see the Beverly Park gates to the left and the right (a north and south gate); however, entry is not possible without an invitation.

Diane Ladd 37

2241 Betty Lane
Beverly Hills, CA 90210

TALL, BLOND, AND COOL, DIANE LADD, MOTHER OF Laura Dern and ex-wife of Bruce Dern, has enjoyed a long career in film, in TV, and on the stage. The star of such movies as *Alice Doesn't Live Here Anymore* and *Wild at Heart*, Ladd purchased this Beverly Hills home in 1993.

This contemporary house, built in 1958, features eleven rooms and a pool. While title records do not reveal a purchase price, the assessed value of the home is $621,316, indicating a market value between $575,000 and $750,000 dollars.

Esther Williams Lamas 38

9377 Readcrest Drive
Beverly Hills, CA 90210

ESTHER WILLIAMS, MGM'S SWIMMING STAR IN THE 1940s, is the widow of Fernando Lamas and stepmother to *Renegades* star Lorenzo Lamas.

Esther Williams Lamas, still very active on the Beverly Hills social circuit, lives in this stately two-story colonial home with eleven rooms, including three bedrooms, three baths, and a pool, off Coldwater Canyon. Williams's longtime residency provides a low tax base on a property worth well over $1.5 million in today's market.

YEAR BUILT: **1963**
LOT SIZE: **20,160 SQ. FT.**
HOME SIZE: **3,086 SQ. FT.**

39 Steve Lawrence Eydie Gorme

820 Greenway Drive
Beverly Hills, CA 90210

GREENWAY DRIVE IS ONE OF THE PREMIER STREETS IN the flats of Beverly Hills. Large, imposing homes face the property of the Los Angeles Country Club, with many homes on the west side of Greenway enjoying golf course vistas.

Popular singing stars Steve Lawrence and Eydie Gorme enjoy life at 820 Greenway. Built in 1948, the two-story contemporary home was remodeled in 1979 and purchased by the Lawrence family in 1983.

The home boasts more than 8,000 square feet, with twenty-one rooms, including five bedrooms, five baths, a spectacular yard, and pool. 820 Greenway is worth in excess of $3 million at today's market value.

40 Jay Leno

1151 & 1149 Tower Road
Beverly Hills, CA 90210

TONIGHT SHOW HOST JAY LENO AND HIS BRIDE, MAVIS, own two homes on Tower Road, forming a compound. 1149 Tower Road is a 2,456-square-foot, one-story contemporary home built in 1957 and purchased by Leno for $55,000 in 1971. It has three bedrooms, three baths.

1151 Tower Road, built in 1978 and purchased by Leno in 1987 for $2,450,000, has five bedrooms and six baths. This much grander home at 6,399 square feet also has a pool.

Chapter Three

Ann-Margret 41

**2727 Coldwater Canyon Drive
Beverly Hills, CA 90210**

THE SWEDISH-BORN ANN-MARGARET OLSSON CAPTURED the American male movie fan in *Viva Las Vegas* (1964), *Bye-Bye Birdie* (1963), and *State Fair* (1962). Some thirty years later, she's still a provocative actress delivering outstanding performances in such films as *Who Will Love My Children?*, *A Streetcar Named Desire* and *The Two Mrs. Grenvilles*.

During the 1960s in her glory days of moviemaking with Elvis Presley, this house on Coldwater Canyon was her residence of choice.

Dean Martin 42

**2002 Loma Vista Drive
Beverly Hills, CA 90210**

DINO CROCETTI, THE LATE CROONER, RAT PACKER, AND movie star known the world over as Dean Martin, lived for a time on swank Loma Vista in a home built in 1967. Martin lived in style at this long, low-slung contemporary villa with seventeen rooms, including five bedrooms, pool, garden, and city-to-ocean view.

LOT SIZE: 37,287 SQ. FT.
HOME SIZE: 10,400 SQ. FT.

43 Steve Martin

9136 Calle Juella
Beverly Hills, CA 90210

ACTOR, PLAYWRIGHT, AND SCREENWRITER STEVE MARTIN hails from Waco, Texas. Martin got a break in television in the 1970s as *Saturday Night Live*'s "wild and crazy guy" and went on to become a box office standout with such films as *Father of the Bride* (1991), *L.A. Story* (1991), *Roxanne* (1987), and *Dead Men Don't Wear Plaid* (1982).

Also a collector of art and lover of fine architecture, Martin has bought and sold residences all over Southern California, including a spectacular concrete modern masterpiece built into a Montecito hillside south of Santa Barbara. That residence, which showcased the actor's contemporary art collection, was sold for a reported price of close to $5 million.

In the spring of 1998, Martin purchased 9136 Calle Juella in Beverly Hills for a reported $3 million plus.

44 Ed McMahon

12000 Crest Court
Beverly Hills, CA 90210

THE FORMER CO-HOST OF *THE TONIGHT SHOW*, HOST OF the syndicated TV show *Star Search*, and representative for Publishers Clearinghouse Sweepstakes, lived in the 1980s behind gates in a traditional estate on Crest Court.

HOME SIZE: 7,013 SQ. FT.
ROOMS: 6 BEDROOMS, 5 BATHS

Chapter Three

Dudley Moore 45
Susan Anton

1853 Noel Place
Beverly Hills, CA 90210

> *ARTHUR* STAR DUDLEY MOORE AND SINGER/ACTRESS Susan Anton are still listed as co-owners of this house, though they have long since divorced. The single-story traditional home with a pool may be seeing more of Anton, though, since Moore lives in Marina del Rey with his present wife.
>
> Built in 1953, this house with wood siding and a shake wood roof has two stories, including fifteen rooms and four bedrooms in a lovely garden setting.

LOT SIZE: 9,100 SQ. FT.
HOME SIZE: 3,862 SQ. FT.

Eddie Murphy 46

2727 Benedict Canyon
Beverly Hills, CA 90210

> THIS PARCEL OF PRIME BEVERLY HILLS CANYON PROPERTY, with a two-story mansion built in 1980 featuring twenty rooms including five bedrooms, was the home of comedic film star and director Eddie Murphy. With credits including *Dr. Dolittle, Coming to America, Trading Places, Beverly Hills Cop,* and *48 Hrs.,* all making millions, Murphy can certainly live the "star" lifestyle.

LOT SIZE: 4 ACRES
HOME SIZE: 10,949 SQ. FT.
ROOMS: 20, WITH 5 BEDROOMS AND 7 BATHS

47 Jack Nicholson

12850 Mulholland Drive
Beverly Hills, CA 90210

WITH HIS NASAL MACHISMO AND SHARP WIT, JACK Nicholson undoubtedly cuts one of the more original figures in the landscape of the later twentieth century. Among his rewards have been three Oscars®—two for Best Actor (*One Flew Over the Cuckoo's Nest*, 1975, and *As Good As It Gets*, 1997) and one for Best Supporting Actor (*Terms of Endearment*, 1983). He has been nominated for an Oscar a whopping eleven times. Meanwhile, he has lived his own life in a contemporary home he has owned for more than thirty years. In a town where some people move as often as they revamp their wardrobes, thirty years is a long time. So long, in fact, that Nicholson is free and clear, owing no mortgage on the home he most likely bought for under $100,000 back in 1969.

Built in 1957, Nicholson's home is stucco, with a gravel roof, ten rooms including four bedrooms, a pool, and a major view.

LOT SIZE: 23,000 SQ. FT
HOME SIZE: 3,303 SQ. FT.

BEVERLY HILLS

Chapter Three 63

Jack Palance 48

1006 Hartford Way
Beverly Hills, CA 90210

BORN WALTER JACK PALAHNUIK ON FEBRUARY 18, 1919, Jack Palance's credits include *City Slickers* (1991), for which he won a Best Supporting Actor Oscar®, *Oklahoma Crude* (1973), *The Desperados* (1969), *The Lonely Man* (1957), and *The Silver Chalice* (1955).

This mansion on Hartford Way, with eighteen rooms including five bedrooms, is behind the Beverly Hills Hotel.

LOT SIZE: **30,492 SQ. FT.**
HOME SIZE: **5,540 SQ. FT**
ASSESSED VALUE: **$1,774,100**

Stefanie Powers 49

2661 Hutton Drive
Beverly Hills, CA 90210

THE GLAMOROUS CO-STAR OF TELEVISION'S LONG-RUNNING *Hart to Hart* series, Stefanie Powers makes her home at 2661 Hutton Drive off Benedict Canyon. Powers has lived in this eight-bedroom, five-bath traditional home, built in 1948 in the tree-shaded canyon surrounding Hutton Drive for at least the past ten years. Hutton Drive has several well-known residents: *Dr. Kildare*'s Richard Chamberlain (who now lives on Oahu) and talk show host Gary Collins and his Miss America bride, Mary Ann Mobley. Statistics on Powers's poolside canyon retreat are impressive.

LOT SIZE: **22,137 SQ. FT.**
HOME SIZE: **3,680 SQ. FT**

50 Elvis Presley

144 Monovale Drive
Beverly Hills, CA 90210

"THE KING" ONCE LIVED AT 144 MONOVALE DRIVE. Built in 1937 in the English style, this home has twenty-five rooms, and Elvis Presley catered to guests with his seven bedrooms and seven bathrooms.

Restored and redone in 1965 before his death, the two-story home's real market value is well over $3 million as it sits on over an acre and a half (69,696 square feet) of golden soil.

The present owner of this estate pays $14,629.28 a year in taxes to live in the house of Elvis.

51 Priscilla Presley

1167 Summit Drive
Beverly Hills, CA 90210

THE GORGEOUS WIDOW OF ELVIS PRESLEY AND THE mother of his only child owns multiple properties on L.A.'s westside. This elegant formal traditional home, with sixteen rooms including six bedrooms as well as gardens and a pool, sits on a winding street of mansions off Benedict Canyon Drive. Presley owns another home in Brentwood, profiled in Chapter Six.

HOUSE SIZE: 5,556 SQ. FT.
PURCHASED BY PRESLEY IN: 1987

Carl Reiner 52

714 North Rodeo Drive
Beverly Hills, CA 90210

THIS BRILLIANT WRITER, ACTOR, TELEVISION PIONEER, AND father of actor/director Rob Reiner lives in the heart of Beverly Hills with his wife, Estelle, who is a frequent entertainer on the national cabaret circuit. Their home on world-famous Rodeo Drive (not the retail shopping section, but the tony residential section north of Santa Monica Boulevard) was built in 1926 when Beverly Hills was just beginning to develop. The two-story colonial home has twenty-two rooms, including seven bedrooms as well as a pool and garden. Current market value: over $3 million.

LOT SIZE: *16,287 SQ. FT.*
HOME SIZE: *5,511 SQ. FT.*

53 Debbie Reynolds

813 Greenway Drive
Beverly Hills, CA 90210

DEBBIE REYNOLDS IS VERY BUSY THESE DAYS TRAVELING the world with her one-woman tour-de-force club act. The little girl from Burbank, who as a young woman starred in major motion pictures, lived here during the 1970s with her former husband Harry Karl (of the store chain) in this very posh residence at 813 Greenway Drive in Beverly Hills.

Karl died, leaving Reynolds near-bankrupt because of his hidden gambling and financial mismanagement of both his and her money. When times were good, they were very good, and the couple lived the high life in a home that today is worth close to $4 million. This handsome French Regency–style home with high ceiling and grand detail, conceived and constructed in the milieu of the International design school, features views of the Los Angeles Country Club and a serene pool and garden.

YEAR BUILT: 1955
LOT SIZE: 35,597 SQ. FT.
HOME SIZE: 8,180 SQ. FT.
ROOMS: 24, WITH 7 BEDROOMS AND 8 BATHS

Smokey Robinson 54

631 North Oakhurst Drive
Beverly Hills, CA 90210

SMOKEY ROBINSON FIRST FORMED THE LEGENDARY *Miracles* while still in high school in 1955. Over the years he has serenaded us with "Cruisin'" and "Being With You." The Motown star made his home for many years at 631 North Oakhurst Drive in the Beverly Hills flats. Built in 1937, the French-style two-story home, with nineteen rooms including five bedrooms as well as a pool, is worth more than $2.5 million in today's market.

LOT SIZE: **14,641** SQ. FT.
HOME SIZE: **6,239** SQ. FT.

George Segal 55

841 Greenway Drive
Beverly Hills, CA 90210

GEORGE SEGAL, THE ACTOR WHO BROKE THROUGH WITH the now classic *Where's Poppa?* and *Who's Afraid of Virginia Woolf?* once lived in this exceptional Spanish-style mansion at 841 Greenway Drive in the posh west-end flats of Beverly Hills. Today it is the property of inventor and art patron Max Palevsky. Built in 1929, the estate features twenty-one rooms, including six bedrooms as well as a pool. Today Segal is a resident of the exclusive Wilshire House, a high-rise condo on the Wilshire Boulevard corridor. When he lived at 841 Greenway, his property was most likely valued between $500,000 and

$800,000 depending on the market. Today the home is worth approximately $4 million.

LOT SIZE: 30,928 SQ. FT.
HOME SIZE: 7,767 SQ. FT.
TAXES: $37,970.12 PER YEAR

56 Dinah Shore
916 Oxford Way
Beverly Hills, CA 90210

ONE OF THE BEST-LOVED STARS OF HER ERA, DINAH Shore came on the Hollywood scene just before World War II and sang her way into the hearts of America for Chevrolet. She lived for many years at 916 Oxford Way, just behind the Beverly Hills Hotel. Shore's one-story sprawling colonial-styled home features sixteen rooms, including seven bedrooms as well as a very large garden with pool and tennis court, enabling Shore, an amateur golfer and a major advocate of women's golf and the title sponsor of the annual Nabisco®/Dinah Shore Tournament in Palm Springs, to indulge in some of her other athletic passions.

LOT SIZE: 39,156 SQ. FT.
HOME SIZE: 5,906 SQ. FT.
ASSESSED VALUE: $2,805,000

Frank Sinatra 57

915 North Foothill Road
Beverly Hills, CA 90210

With his recent passing, Frank Sinatra left his estate at 915 North Foothill Road to his fourth wife of some twenty years, Barbara Marx Sinatra. The magnificent residence next door to the Schacker House, an architectural landmark north of Sunset Boulevard behind impressive iron gates, is valued at more than $5.25 million.

Home Size: 5,544 sq. ft.
Rooms: 22, with 4 bedrooms and 6 baths
Taxes: $54,461.56 per year

Tom Snyder 58

1225 Beverly Estates Terrace
Beverly Hills, CA 90210

Television's inquisitive talk show host, Tom Snyder, purchased this home in 1977 for $76,500. The traditional-style, one-story stucco home with shake wood roof and pool is built in the canyon hillside just east of Benedict Canyon off Beverly Estates Drive. The current market value is close to $1 million.

Lot Size: 12,018 sq. ft.
Home Size: 2,927 sq. ft.
Rooms: 13, with 4 bedrooms and 3.75 baths

★ 59 Jimmy Stewart

918 North Roxbury Drive
Beverly Hills, CA 90210

THE "GOOD GUY" FROM THE CLASSIC FRANK CAPRA FILM *It's a Wonderful Life*, Jimmy Stewart lived out his adult life with wife Gloria in this two-story English country home on a tree-shaded corner double lot in the heart of Beverly Hills. Recently sold by Stewart's children and heirs at a reported figure exceeding $6 million, the residence, built in 1928, has nineteen rooms a pool, and a parklike yard spanning two lots.

LOT SIZE: MORE THAN 1 ACRE
HOME SIZE: 6,367 SQ. FT.

★ 60 Damon Wayans

12089 Summit Circle
Beverly Hills, CA 90210

THE STAR OF *IN LIVING COLOR* AND *DAMON* LIVES IN THIS mansion built in 1988 with seven bedrooms, six baths, and a pool. The estate sits behind private gates at the top of Beverly Hills off Mulholland Drive in an exclusive enclave of custom residences called "The Summit."

HOME SIZE: 9,600 SQ. FT.
PURCHASED BY WAYANS IN: 1993
PURCHASE PRICE: $2,500,000

Chapter Three

Bruce Willis 61
Demi Moore

13511 Mulholland Drive
Beverly Hills, CA 90210

DIE HARD, THE LAST BOY SCOUT, THE PLAYER, PULP Fiction, Armageddon, and many more films have catapulted Bruce Willis into the international spotlight. Demi Moore has fared equally well, with credits including *Ghost, A Few Good Men, Indecent Proposal,* and *G.I. Jane.*

The recently separated couple lived in this modern compound on Mulholland Drive with eleven rooms, including four bedrooms as well as a pool, garden, view, and all the toys their stardom can buy.

HOME SIZE: **2,905** *SQ. FT.*
PURCHASED BY WILLIS AND MOORE IN: **1987**
PURCHASE PRICE: **$1,175,000**

James Woods 62

1612 Gilcrest Drive
Beverly Hills, CA 90120

THE MENACING ACTOR WHO HAS MADE HIS NAME AND his fortune starring in thrillers such as *Casino* (1995), *Against All Odds* (1984), and *The Onion Field* (1979), lived in this small hillside home, built in 1971 with seven rooms including two bedrooms as well as a pool, until 1996, when he sold it for a reported $562,500 dollars.

LOT SIZE: **4,635** *SQ. FT.*
HOME SIZE: **1.766** *SQ. FT.*

63 Pia Zadora
(current owner)
Pickfair – Douglas Fairbanks Jr. & Mary Pickford
(original owners)

1143 Summit Drive
Beverly Hills, CA 90210

THIS PETITE ACTRESS AND SINGER LIVES IN ONE OF Tinseltown's largest mansions. *Pickfair*, named for Mary Pickford and Douglas Fairbanks Jr., was the first movie star home in Beverly Hills, the one that began the show business migration to this territory at the turn of the century. The home was always grand, but not as elaborate as the present version, created by Pia Zadora's estranged husband, financier Meshulam Riklis. More than $20 million transformed the former English-style country house into the massive Italianate palazzo that stands today. Created to house a massive art collection, the new Pickfair is valued at more than $40 million and is very visible from the street on Summit Drive.

HOME SIZE: **25,245** SQ. FT.
ROOMS: **14** BEDROOMS, **24** BATHS
TAXES: **$122,343.28** PER YEAR

BEVERLY HILLS

Chapter Three

Chapter Four

Bel Air

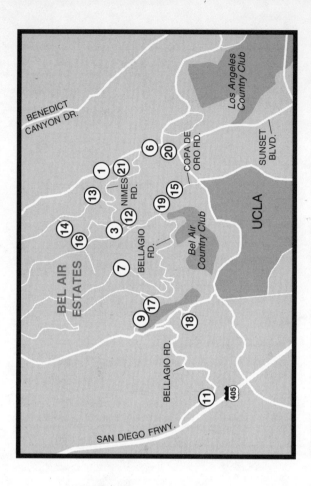

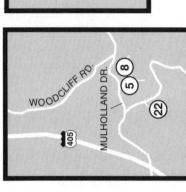
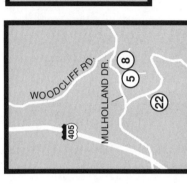

1. DEBBY BOONE/701 N. Beverly Glen Blvd.
2. CHARLES BRONSON/121 Udine Way
3. RED BUTTONS/778 Tortuoso Way
4. JAMES CAAN/1435 Stone Canyon Rd.
5. WILT CHAMBERLIN/15216 Antelo Pl.
6. TOM CRUISE/111 N. Beverly Glen Rd..
7. CLINT EASTWOOD/846 Stradela Rd.
8. FARRAH FAWCETT • RYAN O'NEAL/15229 Antelo Pl.
9. HENRY FONDA/10744 Chalon Rd.
10. PETER FONDA/2179 Linda Flora Dr.
11. JOHN FORSYTHE/11560 Bellagio Rd.
12. ZSA ZSA GABOR/1001 Bel Air Rd.
13. QUINCY JONES/1103 Bel Air Pl.
14. TOM JONES/363 Copa de Oro Rd.
15. BRIAN KEITH/10778 Chalon Rd.
16. KIM NOVAK/780 Tortuoso Way
17. MAUREEN O'HARA/10677 Somma Way
18. LIONEL RICHIE/605 Funchal Rd.
19. TELLY SAVALAS/209 Copa de Oro Rd.
20. JACLYN SMITH/10398 W. Sunset Blvd.
21. ELIZABETH TAYLOR/700 Nimes Rd.
22. JERRY WEST /1210 Moraga Dr.

75

THE BRAINCHILD OF EARLY TWENTIETH-century real estate developer Alphonso Bell, the posh hillside enclave we know today as Bel Air was carved out of the mountains west of Beverly Hills. Here, private residences of significant proportion on large lots surround the heart of Bel Air, the Bel Air Country Club. As it developed, Bel Air came to be synonymous with a more subdued wealth, older money as it were. Whether or not it really was was not important. The Bel Air style is what people have always sought here. Today, Bel Air embodies a very specific look and feeling in residential design. While somewhat difficult to describe, the Bel Air style is at once both warm and formal, and is best displayed in public form in the architecture and the interior design of the Bel Air Hotel on Stone Canyon, north of Sunset Boulevard in the heart of old Bel Air.

Plein-air paintings of California landscape featuring the eucalyptus tree, the Pacific Ocean, and the spring bounty of California's native flora mix with overstuffed furniture upholstered in English prints and tables adorned in chinoiserie finish. This is the mark of the Bel Air Hotel lobby. The Bel Air style is eclectic, studied, and somewhat tailored; a California hybrid of the old conservative eastern seaboard style still fashionable in places such as Greenwich, Rye, and Haverford.

Nancy Reagan brought the Bel Air style to 1600 Pennsylvania Avenue, and today the former first lady and the president are in residence at 668 St. Cloud Road, right next door to the former *Beverly Hillbillies* mansion, which was in fact in the center of Bel Air. The *Hillbillies* estate, now owned by Jerry Parencio, a television financial executive and partner of the prolific Norman Lear, who gave us *All in the Family* and many other shows, paid what was considered a bargain price of some $13 million for the property in the late 1980s. Parencio has invested millions more in refurbishment and changes, including reorienting the main entrance, arguably perhaps the most famil-iar mansion entry in the world via the power of television. Today, celebrity real estate fans can see only hedges. The gates and the drive are gone.

Winding through the narrow streets and green canyons of Bel Air is a true joy, even just for the drive. The homes inspire, the grounds delight the senses. Who knows, you may even pass Tom Cruise and Nicole Kidman jogging down Stone Canyon past the Bel Air Hotel as they often do. That, too, is part of the Bel Air lifestyle, and good reason why so many celebrities, *Fortune* 500 executives, and international personalities including royalty, choose to call Bel Air home.

Chapter Four

Debby Boone 1
701 North Beverly Glen Boulevard
Los Angeles, CA 90077

"YOU LIGHT UP MY LIFE" LANDED PAT BOONE'S DAUGHTER Debby in handsome digs at 701 North Beverly Glen Boulevard. The single-level traditional home, built in 1951, with ten rooms including 4 bedrooms as well as a pool, was sold some time ago to the present owner. Boone called this residence her own in the 1970s.

LOT SIZE: 15,477 SQ. FT.
HOME SIZE: 3,475 SQ. FT.
ASSESSED VALUE TODAY: $733,210

Charles Bronson 2
121 Udine Way
Los Angeles, CA 90077

THIS SPANISH-STYLE ESTATE IN LOWER BEL AIR ON Udine Way, just north of Sunset Boulevard above UCLA, was built in 1936. With twenty-six rooms including ten bedrooms as well as a pool, this was a perfect family retreat for action film star Charles Bronson, best known for movies such as *The Dirty Dozen* (1967), *The Great Escape* (1963), *Kid Galahad* (1962), and *The Magnificent Seven* (1960). Married to the late Jill Ireland in 1968, the couple lived here in the 1980s until they moved to a romantic Mediterranean home in Malibu.

LOT SIZE: 29,176 SQ. FT.
HOME SIZE: 9,397 SQ. FT.
ASSESSED VALUE TODAY: $3,129,732

3 Red Buttons

778 Tortuoso Way
Los Angeles, CA 90077

CLASSIC COMIC RED BUTTONS, "WHO NEVER HAD A PARTY" but did win an Academy Award® for Best Supporting Actor in *Sayonara* (1957), is also known for his role in *The Longest Day* (1962) and a host of other films, TV shows, and plays. He enjoys plenty of socializing with his wife, Alicia, at their swank Bel Air home located at 778 Tortuoso Way off Stone Canyon. Built in 1950, the classic two-story home with twenty-one rooms including five bedrooms as well as a pool, was remodeled in 1969. Today this property, which Buttons purchased in 1986, is worth over $3 million.

LOT SIZE: 2.22 ACRES
HOME SIZE: 5,355 SQ. FT.

4 James Caan

1435 Stone Canyon Road
Los Angeles, CA 90077

TOUGH-GUY ACTOR JAMES "JIMMY" CAAN HAS LIVED ALL over town. One of his most charming homes is located at 1435 Stone Canyon Road in the leafy canyon above the Bel Air Hotel. The star of *The Godfather* (1972), *El Dorado* (1967), and *Lady in a Cage* (1964) lived in this classic house built in 1936. Today, this two-story traditional home with sixteen rooms, including five bedrooms as well as a pool, is worth more than $2 million. At the time Caan lived here, the house, prior to a major 1980 renovation, was worth under $500,000.

LOT SIZE: 32,226 SQ. FT.
HOME SIZE: 5,813 SQ. FT.

Chapter Four

Wilt Chamberlain 5

15216 Antelo Place
Los Angeles, CA 90077

> BASKETBALL LEGEND W. H. CHAMBERLAIN LIVES IN A stylish European villa with doorways and cabinets custom-made to suit his formidable height. He bought this eighteen-room, six-bedroom home in 1969 for $1,215,000. Today the property is worth well over $3 million.

LOT SIZE: *3 ACRES*
HOME SIZE: *7,158 SQ. FT.*

Tom Cruise 6

111 North Beverly Glen Road
Los Angeles, CA 90024

> THIS VERY FORMAL COLONIAL HOME, BUILT IN 1930, WAS once home in the late 1980s to the not-so-formal Tom Cruise, star of *Jerry Maguire* (1997), *Rain Man* (1988), and *Top Gun* (1986).
>
> Today, Cruise and his wife, Nicole Kidman, live in an undisclosed Bel Air location. Ironically, while information on their present residence is not available via public record, the couple are often seen jogging by this old house on Beverly Glen on their way to a good run around nearby Holmby Park at the corner of Beverly Glen and Comstock Avenue.

LOT SIZE: *38,777 SQ. FT.*
HOME SIZE: *8,229 SQ. FT.*
ROOMS: *24, WITH 5 BEDROOMS AND 8 BATHS*
ASSESSED VALUE: *$1,650,113*

7 Clint Eastwood

846 Stradella Road
Los Angeles, CA 90077

THIS OLD-WORLD SPANISH-STYLE RESIDENCE, BUILT IN 1931, has twenty rooms including seven bedrooms in two stories as well as a pool. Eastwood called this mansion home at the time he was making *Every Which Way But Loose* (1978), *The Gauntlet* (1977), *Play Misty for Me* (1971), and *Dirty Harry* (1971). Today the home would be worth over $3 million.

Lot Size: 38,768 sq. ft.
Home Size: 6,136 sq. ft.
Date Sold by Eastwood: 1980
Sale Price: $1,125,000

8 Farrah Fawcett Ryan O'Neal

15299 Antelo Place
Los Angeles, CA 90077

THE ONE-TIME HOME OF RYAN O'NEAL AND FARRAH Fawcett is a modest three-bedroom built in 1950. The two stars lived here when O'Neal made *Irreconcilable Differences* (1984), *What's Up, Doc?* (1972), and *Love Story* (1970), for which he received an Oscar® nomination. They were often seen driving on Sunset Boulevard in their Rolls-Royce® Corniche.

Lot size: 2 acres
Home Size: 2,512 sq. ft.
Assessed Value: $1,071,000

Chapter Four

Henry Fonda 9

10744 Chalon Road
Los Angeles, CA 90077

SHIRLEE A. FONDA, HENRY FONDA'S WIDOW, LIVES IN their Spanish colonial-style home on Chalon, built in 1927. This beautiful old residence with twenty-six rooms, including seven bedrooms as well as a pool is worth more than $4 million in today's real estate market.

Henry Fonda, who passed away August 12, 1982, enjoyed a movie career that spanned decades. Some of his best work includes *On Golden Pond* (1981), *Mister Roberts* (1955), *The Fugitive* (1947), *The Ox-Bow Incident* (1943), *The Lady Eve* (1941), and *Jesse James* (1939).

LOT SIZE: 1 ACRE
HOME SIZE: 9,385 SQ. FT.

Peter Fonda 10

2179 Linda Flora Drive
Los Angeles, CA 90077

ACTOR PETER FONDA IS PART OF A HOLLYWOOD DYNASTY emcompassing his father, Henry, and sister, Jane. The star of *Easy Rider* rose once again into the international spotlight with his Oscar® nomination for *Ulee's Gold* in 1998. Fonda and his wife, Becky, live in a comfortable upper Bel Air home at 2179 Linda Flora Drive, not far from where his father once lived.

LOT SIZE: 18,478 SQ. FT.
HOME SIZE: 3,548 SQ. FT.
PURCHASED BY FONDA IN: 1983
PURCHASE PRICE: $351,000

11 John Forsythe

11560 Bellagio Road
Los Angeles, CA 90049

FORSYTHE, THE HANDSOME TV STAR WHO TRANSCENDED decades and generations from *Bachelor Father* in the 1960s to *Dynasty* in the 1980s, lived with his family until the early 1990s at 11560 Bellagio Road. This large, two-story Connecticut colonial with seventeen rooms, including four bedrooms as well as a view, pool, and sports court, was built in 1940.

LOT SIZE: 27,170 SQ. FT.
HOME SIZE: 4,997 SQ. FT.
ASSESSED VALUE: $1,340, 717

12 Zsa Zsa Gabor

1001 Bel Air Road
Los Angeles, CA 90077

SHE SLAPPED A BEVERLY HILLS POLICEMAN AND THE sound reverberated around the world. The last of the fabulous Gabor sisters of Hungary, Zsa Zsa lives with her prince and current husband at 1001 Bel Air Road. The elegant French-style residence was built in 1955 at the height of young Ms. Gabor's fame, when she made films like *Touch of Evil* (1958), *Lili* (1953), and *Moulin Rouge* (1952).

LOT SIZE: 42,195 SQ. FT.
HOME SIZE: 6,393 SQ. FT.
ROOMS: 12, WITH 4 BEDROOMS AND 5 BATHS

Chapter Four

Quincy Jones 13

1103 Bel Air Place
Los Angeles, CA 90077

A RENAISSANCE MAN IN THE ARENA OF ENTERTAINMENT, with composer credits on films such as *The Color Purple*, *Cactus Flower*, and *The Pawnbroker*. The most nominated artist in Grammy® history with seventy-six nominations and twenty-five wins(!), Jones does it all his own distinct style. The artist, businessman, director, producer, and manager lives in this contemporary home.

LOT SIZE: 26,450 SQ. FT.
HOME SIZE: 14, WITH 4 BEDROOMS, AND 4 BATHS
ASSESSED VALUE: $2,447,000
TAXES: $26,102.85

Tom Jones 14

363 Copa de Oro Road
Los Angeles, CA 90077

THIS IMPOSING ENGLISH MANOR HOUSE AT 363 COPA de Oro Road was the residence of English belter Tom Jones in the 1970s and 1980s. When you see this estate, it looks as if it belongs somewhere in the English countryside. Built in 1940, the mansion has thirty-three rooms, including nine bedrooms, and was recently on the market for an asking price of about $8 million.

LOT SIZE: 43,116 SQ. FT.
HOME SIZE: 11,817 SQ. FT.

15 Brian Keith

**10778 Chalon Road
Los Angeles, CA 90077**

POSSIBLY MOST FAMOUS FOR HIS ROLE AS UNCLE BILL on TV's *Family Affair* in the 1960s, Brian Keith was also a movie star with film credits for *Young Guns* (1988), *Nickelodeon* (1976), *Arrowhead* (1953), and *The Parent Trap* (1961). His Bel Air home at 10778 Chalon Road is presently owned by designer Mossimo Giannulli. This elegant French-Mediterranean–style home, built in 1927, has twenty-three rooms, including seven bedrooms as well as a pool.

*LOT SIZE: **2** ACRES*
*HOME SIZE: **8,935** SQ. FT.*
*PURCHASED BY NEW OWNER IN: **1997***
*ASSESSED VALUE: **$5,151,000***

16 Kim Novak

**780 Tortuoso Way
Los Angeles, CA 90077**

HOLLYWOOD SEX GODDESS KIM NOVAK, NÉE MARILYN Pauline Novak, made movies such as *Kiss Me, Stupid* (1964) and *Boys' Night Out* (1962), and lived during the 1960s in this contemporary one-story home with pool at 780 Tortuoso Way. The house, with thirteen rooms including seven bedrooms, was built in 1952 just as Novak began her rise to stardom.

*LOT SIZE: **34,848** SQ. FT.*
*HOME SIZE: **6,602** SQ. FT.*

Chapter Four

Maureen O'Hara 17

10677 Somma Way
Los Angeles, CA 90077

THIS HANDSOME TRADITIONAL TWO-STORY HOME BUILT IN 1937 with fifteen rooms, including four bedrooms and four baths, was home in the 1960s and 1970s to the incomparable actress Maureen O'Hara. The red-haired beauty starred in such films as *Spencer's Mountain* (1963), *The Parent Trap* (1961), and *Our Man in Havana* (1960).

LOT SIZE: **22,886** SQ. FT.
HOME SIZE: **2,756** SQ. FT.

Lionel Richie 18

605 Funchal Road
Los Angeles, CA 90077

THE HOME THAT LIONEL RICHIE LEFT BEHIND FOLLOWING his divorce from longtime love Brenda is a large, tasteful traditional home with a Spanish-Mediterranean flavor, behind walls and gate at the end of Funchal Road off Bellagio Road in lower Bel Air. The estate, with five bedrooms, maid's quarters, a gorgeous pool, and a garden in a canyon setting, features an enormous formal living room, dining room, and media room. Gleaming hardwood floors, multiple fireplaces, and verdant blooming roses abound. Funchal Road has been home to many celebrities, including Michael J. Fox, who in the 1980s lived just two houses away from Richie in a wonderful French chateau.

19 Telly Savalas

209 Copa de Oro Road
Los Angeles, CA 90077

SAVALAS, BEST KNOW AS THE LOVABLE TV DETECTIVE Kojak, lived during the1980s in this fine home at 209 Copa de Oro Road. Following his passing several years ago, the home was sold for a reported $3,150,000.

The elegant older residence on nearly one acre of prime Bel Air land has twenty-two rooms, including five bedrooms as well as a grand pool.

Savalas was an information officer for the U.S. State Department and an award-winning director for ABC News before embarking—in his late 30s—on an acting career. He was nominated for an Oscar® for his supporting role in 1962's *Birdman of Alcatraz*.

YEAR BUILT: 1927
HOME SIZE: 6,097 SQ. FT.

20 Jaclyn Smith

10398 West Sunset Boulevard
Los Angeles, CA 90077

BEAUTIFUL TV ACTRESS JACLYN SMITH OF *CHARLIE'S Angels* has plenty of room to design her clothing line for Kmart in this $5 million-plus Georgian colonial estate, painted white with dark green trim on the large southeast corner of Sunset Boulevard and Beverly Glen Boulevard.

HOME SIZE: 9,444 SQ. FT.
ROOMS: 22, WITH 6 BEDROOMS, 7 BATHS
SMITH PURCHASED IN: 1992
PURCHASE PRICE: $4,500,000

Chapter Four

Elizabeth Taylor 21

700 Nimes Road
Los Angeles, CA 90077

THE BIGGEST NAME IN TWENTIETH-CENTURY FILMED entertainment is arguably the one and only Elizabeth Taylor, star of *The Taming of the Shrew* (1967), *The Sandpiper* (1965), *Cat on a Hot Tin Roof* (1958), *A Place in the Sun* (1951), and *National Velvet* (1944). Taylor made her home at 700 Nimes Road, a stately two-story traditional built in 1960, with twenty-two rooms, including six bedrooms as well as a pool, about the same time she and Richard Burton were together.

Purchased by Taylor in 1982, the home carries a $2 million mortage on an assessed value amount of $2,809,500. The actual market value is more than $4 million.

LOT SIZE: **1 ACRE**
HOME SIZE: **7,172 SQ. FT.**

22 Jerry West

**1210 Moraga Drive
Los Angeles, CA 90049**

BEL AIR

FORMER BASKETBALL STAR AND PRESENT MANAGING partner and co-owner of the Los Angeles Lakers, Jerry West is a man in the public eye. In his private time, West and his wife, Karen, live at 1210 Moraga Drive, a two-story traditional stucco home built in 1981.

Purchased in 1986 for an unreported figure, today's market value on the home—with basketball hoop and twenty-two rooms—would exceed $2.5 million.

LOT SIZE: 31,359 SQ. FT.
HOME SIZE: 7,927 SQ. FT.
ROOMS: 22, WITH 5 BEDROOMS AND 7 BATHS

Chapter Four

Chapter Five

Holmby Hills
Westwood
Century City

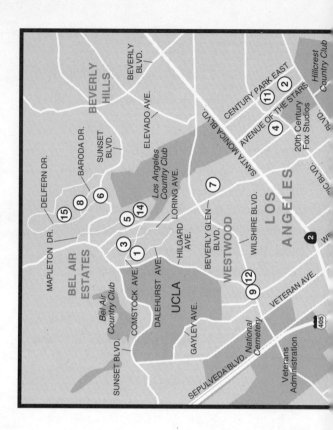

1. JOHN ASTIN/376 Dalehurst Ave.
2. TONI BRAXTON /10120 Empyrean Way
3. LLOYD BRIDGES/225 Loring Ave.
4. CAROL BURNETT/10240 Century Woods Dr.
5. HUGH HEFNER/500 S. Mapleton Dr.
6. ENGELBERT HUMPERDINCK • JANE MANSFIELD/10100 Sunset Blvd.
7. JOHN LITHGOW/1319 Warnall Ave.
8. HENRY MANCINI/261 Baroda Dr.
9. AUSTIN PECK/10375 Wilshire Blvd.
10. MICHELLE PHILLIPS/10557 Troon Ave.
11. VIDAL SASSOON/2112 Century Park Lane
12. TOM SELLECK/10560 Wilshire Blvd.
13. AARON SPELLING/594 S. Mapleton Dr.
14. CONNIE STEVENS/243 Delfern Dr.

ALPHONSO BELL, CREATOR OF BEL AIR, worked closely with partners Arthur Letts, a millionaire businessman who founded the Broadway department stores among other projects, and the Jans Brothers, a team of architectural real estate developers responsible for development of much of the Westside, including Westwood Village adjacent to UCLA. Together they created the residential neighborhood of Westwood, Holmby Hills, Little Holmby Hills, and what is affectionately known as "Baby" Bel Air, a tract of smart-looking homes just south of Sunset Boulevard and just east of the San Diego Freeway, built in the post-war boom, adjacent to the estates of old Bel Air.

All of this activity began in the early 1920s and continued well into the late 1960s and even 1970s as the now cosmopolitan adventure called Century City took shape adjacent to Westwood and Beverly Hills. Soon, a new trend turned the once low-rise profile of Los Angeles into a major metropolis. The high-rise apartments and a thing called the condo began to transform Wilshire Boulevard, in Century City and Westwood, into a condo-mania high-rise configuration of lifestyles that is today referred to as simply "The Corridor." It is home to many a personality that has disposed of single-family quarters in favor of views and valet service. The two most celebrity-studded of the many fine buildings, all of which contain a roster of well-known names, are the Wilshire House located at the northwest corner of Wilshire and Westholme, and the tall, slender Wilshire with its impressive old-world copper roof almost directly across the street.

In Century City proper, where you'll find the Shubert Theater, ABC Entertainment Center, Century Plaza Hotel, and Century City Shopping Center, one of the first urban upscale shopping malls in the nation, you will also find very exclusive condominium living with buildings such as the I.M. Pei-designed Century Towers, home to the Robert Wise family. Wise produced *The Sound of Music* among other great motion pictures. A number of famous residents live at nearby Le Parc and Century Hill, which includes the Southern California residence of Governor Pete Wilson and the part-time homes of stars like Carol Burnett, who splits her time between other parts of the nation during the year.

The most exclusive, however, of all these Westside regions is the community of Holmby Hills. Sandwiched between Beverly Hills to the east, Bel Air to the north, and Westwood to the west, this relatively small patch of very rich dirt is home to some of the biggest names in every field. The homes match the egos and the bank

Chapter Five

balances. Arthur Letts set the standard by building his English brick manor that today serves as home to another uniquely American original, Hugh Hefner. Now known as the Playboy Mansion, the Letts estate is a grand baronial mansion in the most old-world European tradition, set on Charing Cross Road just below Sunset Boulevard, near the intersection of Mapleton Drive.

Some of the house and grounds are visible from the front on Charing Cross Road. However, a better view can be had by driving around the back onto Mapleton, where one can see much more, especially when the massive gates open for deliveries. Don't try and sneak in. Old-world ambiance ends and twenty-first–century security takes over at the gates.

Perhaps the most impressive residence in a community of drop-dead celebrity homes is the mansion built by Aaron and Candy (Carole) Spelling at the corner of South Mapleton and Clubview Drive. It's a limestone manor in the French Regency style set on a five-acre promontory that was once home to Bing and Dixie Crosby. The Spellings paid $5 million for the old Crosby home, then razed it. They wanted the site. And on that site they spent a reported $40 million plus to create the house that *Charlie's Angels* and other television shows financed.

One final note of interest concerning many of the mansions of Holmby Hills, Bel Air, Beverly Hills, and the entire region. Some of the best were designed in the 1930s and 1940s by an African-American architect named Paul Williams. At a time when black Americans were still living in segregated communities for the most part, a black man was one of the most respected designers of his time, building homes for some of the most influential people of his day. Los Angeles continues to earn its reputation for opportunity, for surprise, for constant flux and change. Here's a look at some of the adventure seekers who have called Westwood, Holmby Hills, and Century City home.

John Astin 1

376 Dalehurst Avenue
Los Angeles, CA 90024

THE FORMER HOME OF *ADDAMS FAMILY* DAD JOHN Astin, former husband of Patty Duke, is anything but creepy. This smart colonial-style residence, built in 1941, is a $1.5 million home with fifteen rooms, including four bedrooms as well as a pool, on a beautiful tree-lined street. Astin sold the property to the present owner in 1995 for a reported $904,545.

LOT SIZE: *20,369 SQ. FT.*
HOME SIZE: *3,993 SQ. FT.*

Toni Braxton 2

10120 Empyrean Way
Los Angeles, CA 90067

THIS YOUNG SINGER WITH A STRING OF TOP 40 HITS lives in a swank Century City condo on Empyrean Way. With another home in New York City, Toni Braxton spends her L.A. time in this spacious two-bedroom, three-bath condo with 2,306 square feet of living space. The complex, built in 1979, is a major security building with full amenities. Braxton reportedly purchased the condo in 1996 for $725,000.

3 Lloyd Bridges

225 Loring Avenue
Los Angeles, CA 90024

THE WORLD LOST ONE OF ITS MOST ADMIRED ACTORS with the recent passing of Lloyd Bridges. Bridges, who starred in the TV series *Sea Hunt*, and his wife, Dorothy, raised their three children—actors Beau and Jeff and daughter Susan—in this traditional, stone-faced two-story colonial in a neighborhood referred to as "Little Holmby."

Built in 1936, this home has twenty-five rooms, including five bedrooms, and faces Loring Avenue, one of the prettiest streets in the Westwood–Little Holmby area. The market value of the Bridges home is more than $1.75 million.

LOT SIZE: 13,935 SQ. FT.
HOME SIZE: 4,830 SQ. FT.

HOLMBY HILLS / WESTWOOD / CENTURY CITY

Carol Burnett 4

10240 Century Woods Drive
Century City, CA 90067

THE WARM AND GRACIOUS FUNNY LADY OF TV FAME, Carol Burnett, host of her own decade-long show on CBS, lives in a gated community of fewer than twenty-five homes built in a hedged and tree-protected compound known as Century Woods.

Originally a condominium development built in low-rise form in the 1980s, the newer residences of Century Woods were built in the early 1990s in the Mediterranean style to offer those who wanted a single-family home without maintenance and excessive yardwork, an alternative to living in a condo building.

Burnett, who has lived all over the Westside in everything from bungalows to mansions to a high-rise apartment, chose a stylish Mediterranean home with spacious rooms and fine finishes including handmade tile and hardwood floors. This Westside abode, walking distance from Century City shopping, dining, and entertainment, has 4,000 feet of living space and is worth close to $3 million on today's market.

⭐ 5 Hugh Hefner

500 South Mapleton Drive
Los Angels, CA 90024

ONE OF THE GREAT ESTATES OF L.A., THIS EXQUISITE English Tudor manor house, built in 1929, took on an entirely new set of standards when Hugh Hefner made it the Playboy Mansion. Hefner, who has owned this estate for many years, refinanced the mansion in 1996, taking out a new first trust deed in the amount of $6,700,000. Given the home's style and spaciousness, with twenty-four rooms and five bedrooms as well as the all-time incredible gardens, grotto, pool, tennis court and more, the market value of the estate today surely exceeds $20 million.

⭐ 6 Engelbert Humperdink
(most recent celebrity owner)
Jayne Mansfield
(previous celebrity owner)

10100 Sunset Boulevard
Los Angeles, CA 90077

THIS ENORMOUS AND VERY PINK MEDITERRANEAN HOME, very visible off Sunset Boulevard, features a heart-shaped swimming pool and grand living spaces. The estate once belonged to actress Jayne Mansfield, and more recently to Engelbert Humperdinck.

Chapter Five

John Lithgow 7
1319 Warnall Avenue
Los Angeles, CA 90024

HE EPITOMIZES THE THIRTYSOMETING GENERATION THAT IS now facing fifty. John Lithgow, star of TV's *3rd Rock From the Sun*, and such films as *Cliffhanger* (1993) *Terms of Endearment* (1983)—for which he received an Oscar® nomination—and his wife, Mary, call 1319 Warnall Avenue home. This modest Spanish-style home, built in 1933 with fourteen rooms, including five bedrooms, rests in a lovely family neighborhood in Westwood. Purchased by Lithgow in 1984 for $500,000, today the home would approach $900,000 at current market rates.

Lot Size: **8,407 sq. ft.**
Home Size: **3,858 sq. ft.**

Henry Mancini 8
261 Baroda Drive
Holmby Hills, CA 90077

HE GAVE US "MOON RIVER" AND "TWO FOR THE ROAD." The incomparable Henry Mancini, prolific songwriter, composer, and film scorer with credits for *The Pink Panther* theme, and *Breakfast at Tiffany's*, lived with his wife, Ginny, up until his death several years ago, in this exceptional European villa in the English country style on Baroda Drive, north of Sunset Boulevard in prime Holmby Hills.

Following his passing, Mancini's wife sold this property for nearly $5 million. It included a baronial-sized living room with a vaulted and beamed ceiling, tennis court, pool, offices, and motor court.

9 Austin Peck
10375 Wilshire Boulevard
Los Angeles, CA 90024

DARK-HAIRED, DARING YOUNG LEADING MAN AUSTIN Peck has spent the past three years charming viewers of the NBC daytime drama *Days of Our Lives*. Peck, who also happens to be a boxer and a cartoonist, comes from New York City.

This rising young star lives in an older Wilshire Boulevard condo built in 1958. The 832-sqare feet, one-bedroom, two-bath unit was purchased in 1992 for an undisclosed sale price.

Michelle Phillips 10

**10557 Troon Avenue
Los Angeles, CA 90064**

MICHELLE PHILLIPS CAME INTO THE SPOTLIGHT AS A member of the Mamas and the Papas with husband John Phillips in the late 1960s. The group brought us "Monday, Monday," "Dream a Little Dream of Me," and "Words of Love." For eight days in 1970, Phillips was married to wild-man actor Dennis Hopper. She became an actor, with notable roles in the movies *Dillinger* and *The Taming of the Shrew*. Phillips also was a cast member of the TV series *Knots Landing*. The mother of actress Mackenzie Phillips and singer Chynna Phillips (Chynna has gained fame as a member of the pop trio Wilson Phillips), Michelle does her "California Dreamin'" these days in a lovely Spanish-style bungalow. Built in 1928, the home features a stucco exterior and nine rooms, including two bedrooms, as well as a Jacuzzi in the backyard.

LOT SIZE: 5,737 SQ. FT
HOME SIZE: 1,777 SQ. FT.
PURCHASED BY PHILLIPS IN: 1992
ASSESSED VALUE: $258,000

11 Vidal Sassoon

2112 Century Park Lane
Los Angeles, CA 90067

MASTER OF HAIR VIDAL SASSOON HAS LIVED IN A BEVY of beautiful homes all over the Westside of L.A., from major mansions to this condo on Century Park Lane in Century City. Sassoon purchased this 1,300-square-foot unit with two bedrooms, two baths in 1986.

12 Tom Selleck

10560 Wilshire Boulevard
Los Angeles, CA 90024

LEADING MAN TOM SELLECK OF *MAGNUM P.I.* FAME scored a hit with his performance in the big-screen comedy *In and Out*. Born and raised in Los Angeles, the athletic actor has owned homes in both the San Fernando Valley and in the city. Presently this luxury condo on Wilshire Boulevard is his in-town address.

Selleck purchased this two-bedroom, three-bath unit with 1,828 square feet and a commanding view for $350,000. The building, built in 1982 and known as the "10-5-60," is one of the finer addresses on the Wilshire corridor.

Aaron Spelling 13

**549 South Mapleton Drive
Holmby Hills, CA 90024**

THIS IS THE GRANDFATHER OF ALL L.A. MANSIONS. Aaron and Candy (Carole) Spelling's exquisite French limestone palace on five Holmby Hills acres overlooking the Los Angeles Country Club and Holmby Park, represents the ultimate 1980s real estate indulgence. You can drive by 549 South Mapleton Drive, but please keep your tongue in your mouth and your hands on the wheel. The creator of TV's *Beverly Hills, 90210* and dozens of TV hits over the past three decades, lives in a home with a market value of more than $50 million with some experts asserting a $75 million to $100 million price tag.

HOME SIZE: 52,503 SQ. FT.
ROOMS: TOO MANY TO COUNT, WITH 11 BEDROOMS,
9 BATHS, AND MULTIPLE STAFF QUARTERS
TAXES: $351,710.04 PER YEAR

14 Connie Stevens

243 Delfern Drive
Los Angeles, CA 90077

ACTRESS AND SINGER CONNIE STEVENS, FORMER WIFE of Eddie Fisher, lives in a very elegant colonial mansion built in 1939 with thirty-one rooms, including seven bedrooms as well as a pool. The current market value exceeds $5 million.

In a career that has spanned more than three decades, Stevens, who debuted at age sixteen in a singing group called The Three Debs, rocketed to fame in the early 1960s with a Warner Bros.' recording called "Kookie, Kookie (Lend Me Your Comb)." Film roles followed in *Young and Dangerous, Party Crashers,* and *Rock-A-Bye Baby.*

Her national fame was cemented when Stevens became Cricket Blake in the TV series *Hawaiian Eye* on ABC. Other film and TV credits include *Palm Springs Weekend, Grease 2, Back to the Beach, Wendy and Me, Murder She Wrote,* and *The Love Boat.*

Stevens has also starred on Broadway in Neil Simon's *Star Spangled Girl* and has been a headliner in Las Vegas and worldwide for the past twenty years. In recent times, Stevens has launched a successful skin care line known as Forever Spring. She is also well known for her work with animals, the physically other-abled, and Native Americans through her project Windfeather, which raises funds to send Native American youth to college.

Chapter Five

Chapter Six

Brentwood

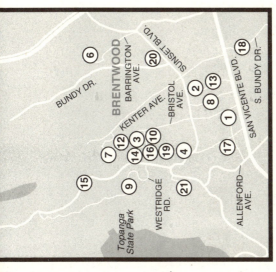

1. ROSEANNE BARR/12916 Evanston St.
2. JAMES BELUSHI/12323 Helena Dr.
3. JOAN CRAWFORD/426 N. Bristol Ave.
4. PHYLISS DILLER/153 N. Rockingham Ave.
5. MICHAEL DOUGLAS/2915 Mandeville Cyn. Rd.
6. HARRISON FORD/655 MacCoulloch Dr.
7. JAMES GARNER/33 Oakmont Dr.
8. TOM HANKS/321 S. Anita Ave.
9. NORMAN LEAR/1911 & 1899 Westridge Dr.
10. HAL LINDEN/416 S. Bristol Ave.
11. FRED MacMURRAY/485 Malvern Ave.
12. STEVE McQUEEN & ALI McGRAW/27 Oakmont Dr.
13. MARILYN MONORE/12305 5th Helena Dr.
14. MICHAEL OVITZ/457 N. Rockingham Ave.
15. GREGORY PECK/2359 Mandeville Cyn. Rd.
16. COLE PORTER/416 N. Rockingham Ave.
17. ROB REINER/12940 Hanover St.
18. NICOLE BROWN SIMPSON/875 S. Bundy Dr.
19. O.J. SIMPSON/360 N. Rockingham Ave.
20. SALLY STRUTHERS/181 N. Saltair Ave.
21. ROBERT WAGNER/1500 Old Oak Rd. & 1505 Old Oak Rd.

107

UNTIL 1994, BRENTWOOD, A RESIDENtial section of West Los Angeles bordering Santa Monica and the beach, was the epitome of understatement. Brentwood wanted it that way. But a man they once adored, for the most part, changed all of that. O. J. Simpson, Heisman Trophy winner, famous USC football player, and resident of 360 North Rockingham in tony Brentwood Park, put an end to the silence in his neighborhood. The murder of his former wife, Nicole Brown Simpson, and her friend Ronald Goldman turned Brentwood into a circus of news crews, helicopters, gawkers, and trial watchers. After the gruesome murders and ensuing court battle that captivated the world, Brentwood is on the map as the place where O. J. lived and Nicole died.

It also happens to be one of the most beautiful spots on earth, with a perfect climate cooled by soft Santa Monica sea breezes. Old trees send their formidable branches in all directions throughout Brentwood. In fact, the main thoroughfare, called San Vicente Boulevard, is lined with a parkway featuring lawns and a procession of the California Coral Tree (the State Tree of the Golden State). The magnificent tree, with its gnarly trunk and branches, sends forth a flower of impressive dimension in a color best described as luscious cinnabar and coral. San Vicente is the avenue of joggers, both celebrity and noncelebrity in status, as one might see a host of famous faces including the likes of TV star Mark Harmon making his way to the ocean at the end of the boulevard.

Brentwood became the celebrity address du jour in the 1980s as many younger stars chose to pass on the changing Beverly Hills scene. Actually, Brentwood had always had its contingent. Gregory Peck, Pat O'Brien, Julie Andrews and Blake Edwards, and many other stars had long called the idyllic coastal community home. Brentwood had always been expensive and chic, but in a less ostentatious way than neighboring Bel Air, Holmby Hills, and Beverly Hills. It was also a bit horsey, featuring mini-ranches in an area known as Sullivan Canyon just north of Sunset Boulevard and west of Mandeville Canyon. Today, stars such as Robert Wagner, who lives on Old Ranch Road with wife, Jill St. John, love the atmosphere of country in the city.

The most posh and expensive neighborhood in Brentwood is called the Park, or Brentwood Park to be precise. It is an area defined by Rockingham on the west end, where homes sit on what is called the rim, overlooking Riviera Country Club, out to the Pacific Ocean. On the east, Cliffwood Drive marks the perimeter of the park that stretches between San Vicente to the south and above Sunset to an area known as Oakmont Drive to the far north. Oakmont Drive, at the top of Rockingham, is a private road that does not permit public access. Stars such as Steve McQueen, Audrey Hepburn, and members of the singing Jackson family have called Oakmont home.

Despite the Simpson murders, Brentwood is still the most sought-after residential real estate on the Westside. Preferred by celebs and leaders of business for its quiet and private lifestyle, 90049 is the zip code for those in the know seeking a special quality of life in one of the biggest and most pressure-filled cities on earth.

And by the way, if you're into seeing your favorite star at his or her most relaxed, check out the chicken barbeque take-out at the Brentwood Country Mart at the corner of San Vicente and 26th Street. You'll see more stars than in any fancy restaurant sitting around the fire pit, having coffee, reading the daily trade papers, *The Hollywood Reporter* and *Variety,* and maybe even indulging in a few scrumptious French fries dipped in homemade barbecue sauce to go along with a chicken wing or two, diet permitting.

1 Roseanne Barr

12916 Evanston Street
Brentwood, CA 09949

For a time, at the top of her series fame, Roseanne owned two homes side by side in posh Brentwood Park. Her main residence was a 1980s version of an English Tudor mansion on Evanston Street. The second home, a classic brick-fronted Georgian colonial at the southwest corner of Evanston and Burlingame, united the two properties into a compound. An interesting footnote is that Roseanne actually re-joined the two homes into one estate, as they had been for decades until the prior owner of the colonial home on the corner subdivided the estate, turning half of the backyard into what eventually became Roseanne's primary residence. Trouble in paradise prompted the brash comedienne to list and sell the colonial on the corner for a reported $3 million-plus figure. The Evanston Street Tudor, visible from the street in spite of walls, gates, and shrubs, is a large home with pool, tennis court, and every toy imaginable for Roseanne's kids. The Evanston property, because of the tennis court, commanded a sale price of more than $4 million.

Chapter Six

James Belushi 2
12323 Helena Drive #12
Brentwood, CA 90049

The Helenas are a most charming and popular set of streets off Carmelina Avenue in Brentwood. Arranged like the spokes of a comb, the numerically ordered Helenas shoot off a central avenue. Jim Belushi, co-star of *Curly Sue* (1991), *About Last Night* (1986) and *Thief* (1981), lives on Helena 12 at 12323.

The actor's home is Spanish colonial in design, dating from 1928 and known in architectural guides as "The Hamilton House," designed by John Byers with Edla Muir. On a relatively average size lot, the ten-room, four-bedroom residence has a pool, garden, and tile roof. Today's market value is close to $1 million.

Lot Size: 8,538 sq. ft.
Home Size: 2,659 sq. ft.

⭐ 3 Joan Crawford

426 North Bristol Avenue
Los Angeles, CA 90049

SUPERSTAR OF THE '30s, '40s, AND '50s, JOAN CRAWFORD, Oscar® winner for her role in *Mildred Pierce* (1945), lived in grand style on North Bristol Avenue in Brentwood Park. Crawford also lived at various times in spectacular homes in Bel Air, Holmby Hills, and at 181 North Saltair in Brentwood. (See Sally Struthers for more on this house.) One of the most impressive streets in Los Angeles, North Bristol is also home to Los Angeles Mayor Richard Riordan. Mayor Riordan owns a spectacular Italian villa on manicured, gated grounds at the northwest corner of North Bristol and Bristol Circle, just above Sunset Boulevard.

⭐ 4 Phyllis Diller

153 North Rockingham Avenue
Los Angeles, CA 90049

HOMES ON THE "ROCKINGHAM RIM" RANGE FROM A low of $2 million plus to well over $10 million.

Comedienne Phyllis Diller, who made her show business name making fun of her husband, "Fang," lives in a wonderful old-world European villa perched on parklike grounds on North Rockingham.

A clear view of this beautiful home awaits the drive-by visitor searching for class, quality, and natural beauty in star homes. Diller's estate exceeds $5 million in value.

Chapter Six

Michael Douglas 5

2915 Mandeville Canyon Road
Brentwood, CA 90049

RECENTLY DIVORCED SUPERSTAR MICHAEL DOUGLAS, STAR of *Disclosure* (1994), *Basic Instinct* (1989), and *Wall Street* (1987), lived with his wife in this spectacular mansion. The new bachelor divides his time between family in Santa Barbara, West Los Angeles, and the East Coast. One of his former L.A. haunts is the home on Mandeville Canyon Road in Brentwood.

Harrison Ford 6

655 MacCulloch Drive
Brentwood, CA 90049

TODAY'S BIGGEST MALE BOX OFFICE DRAW, HARRISON Ford, star of *Six Days, Seven Nights* (1998), *Air Force One* (1997), *Blade Runner* (1982), and the *Star Wars* and *Indiana Jones* trilogies, began his adulthood as a carpenter. Today with his wife, screenwriter Melissa Mathison, Ford has homes in Beverly Hills, Brentwood, and the mountains of Montana. One of their properties, which they purchased in 1983 for $1 million, is this contemporary, substantial but not showy house on MacCulloch Drive in Brentwood.

LOT SIZE: 34,412 SQ. FT.
HOME SIZE: 6,674 SQ. FT.
ROOMS: 9, WITH 2 BEDROOMS AND 5 BATHS

7 James Garner

33 Oakmont Drive
Los Angeles, CA 90049

JAMES GARNER, PERHAPS BEST KNOWN FOR HIS TELEvision role as Jim Rockford, in *The Rockford Files,* also enjoyed quite a career in films, starring in such movies as *Murphy's Romance* (1985), *Grand Prix* (1966), and *The Americanization of Emily* (1964).

During the 1970s, Garner lived on a semiprivate street known as Oakmont at the northern edges of Brentwood Park. His contemporary home, constructed in 1966, has sixteen rooms, including three bedrooms as well as a pool. The property is worth more than $2 million.

LOT SIZE: 36,155 SQ. FT.
HOME SIZE: 4,356 SQ. FT.

8 Tom Hanks

321 South Anita Avenue
Brentwood, CA 90049

The Oscar®-winning star of *Saving Private Ryan* (1998), *Apollo 13* (1995), *Forrest Gump* (1994), *Sleepless in Seattle* (1993), *Philadelphia* (1993), and *Big* (1988) lived during the 1980s with his wife, Rita Wilson, in a charming home on Brentwood's Anita Avenue. The older stucco house is south of Sunset Boulevard on a tree-lined street of families with kids and golden retrievers. Most of the homes in this neighborhood are in the $1 million-plus range, with land and space at a premium.

Norman Lear 9

1911 & 1899 Westridge Road
Brentwood, CA 90049

FOLLOWING HIS DIVORCE FROM LONGTIME LOVE, Frances, Norman Lear sold the Brentwood Park estate that he had earned with a string of television hits that began in 1970 with *All in the Family*. The prolific writer headed north into the hills above Brentwood's Mandeville Canyon and purchased land on which to build his new dream home. Several years and some $10 million later, 1911 and 1899 Westridge Road display the estate of Norman Lear. Wind up the canyon road and prepare yourself for a treat at the top.

1899 WESTRIDGE ROAD
YEAR BUILT: 1970
LOT SIZE: 17,017 SQ. FT.
HOME SIZE: 1,937 SQ. FT.
ROOMS: 2 BEDROOMS, 2 BATHS

1911 WESTRIDGE ROAD
YEAR BUILT: 1985
LOT SIZE: 330,990 SQ. FT.
HOME SIZE: 13,320 SQ. FT.
ROOMS: 7 BEDROOMS, 15 BATHS WITH POOL

10 Hal Linden

416 South Bristol Avenue
Brentwood, CA 90049

BARNEY MILLER DID ALL RIGHT FOR HIMSELF. HAL LINDEN, song-and-dance man and TV policeman, lives with his wife, Frances, on South Bristol Avenue in the heart of Brentwood park, just north of San Vicente Boulevard.

Exquisitely redone in the 1980s, the Linden residence, built in 1930, features thirteen rooms, four bedrooms, and a lovely pool and garden. The market value of the Linden home today exceeds $2.8 million.

LOT SIZE: 21,998 SQ. FT.
HOME SIZE: 4,418 SQ. FT.

11 Fred MacMurray

485 Malvern Avenue
Los Angeles, CA 90049

FRED MACMURRAY, THE LOVABLE SINGLE DAD IN TELEvision's long-running *My Three Sons*, also starred in films such as *Double Indemnity* (1944), *No Time for Love* (1943), and *The Texas Ranger* (1936). The son of a concert violinist, he started out as a band saxophonist and vocalist to pay his way through Carroll College in Wisconsin.

Married in 1954 to actress June Haver, Fred lived in a traditional home with his bride until the 1980s on Brentwood's Malvern Drive.

Chapter Six

Steve McQueen 12
Ali McGraw

27 Oakmont Drive
Los Angeles, CA 90049

>Terrence Steven McQueen died November 7, 1980. He made his film debut with a small part in *Somebody Up There Likes Me* (1956) and went on to become a major box office star in action films such as *Papillon* (1973), *The Getaway* (1972), *Bullitt* (1968), and *The Great Escape* (1963).
>
>McQueen, at the time he was married to actress Ali McGraw, lived on Brentwood's Oakmont Drive in the 1970s, on a private street at the top of Rockingham Drive in a contemporary home with plenty of garage space for his hot rods. The residence with pool would be worth more than $3 million on today's market.

Marilyn Monroe 13

12305 5th Helena Drive
Brentwood, CA 90049

>Perhaps the most famous of the Helena residents was Marilyn Monroe. She lives and died at 12305 5th Helena, just south of Sunset Boulevard off Carmelina Avenue.
>
>Her Spanish-style, one-story bungalow stands today much as it did nearly forty years ago when the star of *Some Like It Hot* and other classic films inhabited the house. Neither grand nor special in any way, the cozy three-bedroom home was not adorned with "star" accoutrements in Monroe's day either.

She was, by many accounts, a woman of simple tastes, owning no jewelry or wardrobe to speak of. Everything was on loan to promote her work and image. In Monroe's own words, "I just want to be wonderful." Nothing else mattered.

Check out 12305 5th Helena. It's quite visible over a fence. You'll be surprised at the peaceful simplicity of the home of the once frenetic, complicated soul who still is very much alive today in Americans' hearts.

14 Michael Ovitz
457 North Rockingham Avenue
Brentwood, CA 90049

INASMUCH AS THIS IS THE AGE OF THE SUPERDEAL as well as the superstar, one man above all others has achieved international recognition as the supernegotiator.

Co-founder of Creative Artists Agency (CAA) and former Disney executive who left the company with a multi million—dollar exit visa, Michael Ovitz lives with his family on North Rockingham Avenue.

Elegant best describes this traditional colonial estate. Built in 1937 and completely remodeled and upgraded by the Ovitz family, the two-story house has twenty-seven rooms, including seven bedrooms and eight baths as well as a beautiful garden with a pool. The market value of this property exceeds $6 million.

LOT SIZE: 28,691 SQ. FT.
HOME SIZE: 8,339 SQ. FT.

Chapter Six

Gregory Peck 15

**2359 Mandeville Canyon Road
Brentwood, CA 90049**

BORN IN LA JOLLA, CALIFORNIA, IN 1916, GREGORY PECK thought as a young man that he would become a doctor. Instead, he found his way into acting. He began on the Broadway stage in 1942 with a role in *The Morning Star* and landed back in California in 1944 to work on screen for RKO Pictures in *Glory Days*.

Other impressive credits include *Arabesque* (1966), *To Kill a Mockingbird* (1962), *On the Beach* (1959), *Duel in the Sun* (1947), and *Gentleman's Agreement* (1947). For many years, Peck's residence of choice has been 2359 Mandeville Canyon, north of Sunset Boulevard approximately two miles up the canyon.

The handsome star and his family lived in this very traditional colonial home with wood siding, a heavy shake roof, and accents of brick and stone. The property features a private yard with pool and gardens, including a lush lawn shaded by the early setting afternoon sun.

16 Cole Porter

**416 North Rockingham Avenue
Los Angeles, CA 90049**

THE MAN WHO ENTERTAINED LAVISHLY AND DEFINED romantic music and much of the lifestyle of the Jazz Age in America, was composer Cole Porter, whose primary residence was in New York City. He also owned property in Brentwood in the 1930s. This charming English-style home was built in 1926 with stucco-and-wood siding and a wood shingle roof. The home has fourteen rooms, including five bedrooms, and a current market value of more than $3 million.

LOT SIZE: 22,913 SQ. FT.
HOME SIZE: 5,970 SQ. FT

17 Rob Reiner

**12940 Hanover Street
Los Angeles, CA 90049**

BUILT IN 1936, THIS CHARMING 6,962-SQUARE-FOOT home in prime Brentwood Park is the residence of Rob Reiner and family. Purchased in 1991 for a reported $4,750,000, the property is quite a pad for the guy who became famous as "Meathead" on television's *All In the Family*. Today Reiner, whose father is the legendary Hollywood veteran Carl Reiner, is a very successful actor and director of films, including *When Harry Met Sally* (1989) and *A Few Good Men* (1992).

Chapter Six

Nicole Brown Simpson 18

875 South Bundy Drive
Brentwood, CA 90049

> The condo that shook the world has been sold, and the entrance off Bundy Drive redesigned to offer some peace to the victims of the murder and to the residents of the complex.

O. J. Simpson 19

360 North Rockingham Avenue
Los Angeles, CA 90049

> Sold in a foreclosure auction for nearly $3 million, O. J. Simpson's Brentwood estate was recently demolished.

Sally Struthers 20

181 North Saltair Avenue
Brentwood, CA 90049

> Recently sold for a figure reported to be close to $3 million, the Brentwood residence of television and stage star Sally Struthers has quite the Hollywood pedigree. Originally built in the late 1930s by studio mogul, Jesse L. Lasky, 181 Saltair was also home at one time to Joan Crawford. Struthers and her former husband, TV psychiatrist Dr. William Rader, purchased the French

colonial estate in the late 1970s as their family residence. The brick home with a guest house, six-car garage, and massive backyard filled with enormous trees, roses, and specimen plants of all California varieties, has more than twenty grand old rooms with wonderful architectural detail.

Struthers, after selling this home and going on the road to star in the Broadway musical *Annie*, purchased another Hollywood residence with a 1920s pedigree for herself, her daughter, and her beloved menagerie of pets.

21 Robert Wagner
1500 Old Oak Road
Brentwood, CA 90049

ROBERT WAGNER, A SOUTHERN CALIFORNIA NATIVE SON who began a film career against his family's wishes and ended up one of the biggest stars of the small screen, lives today with his wife, Jill St. John, at 1500 Old Oak Road in Brentwood's Mandeville Canyon. Wagner purchased this sixteen-room, six-bedroom ranch house several years ago following the untimely and tragic death of his first wife, Natalie Wood, leaving their home on Canon Drive in the flats of Beverly Hills.

YEAR BUILT: 1940
LOT SIZE: 41,121 SQ. FT.
HOME SIZE: 4,556 SQ. FT.

WAGNER ALSO OWNS THE HOME NEXT DOOR AT 1505 OLD OAK. BUILT IN 1946, THE 2,448-SQUARE-FOOT RESIDENCE ON A 28,488-SQUARE-FOOT PAD SERVES AS ADDITIONAL SPACE FOR THE WAGNER/ST. JOHN FAMILY. THE MARKET VALUE OF BOTH PROPERTIES PUT TOGETHER WOULD BE MORE THAN $5 MILLION.

Chapter Seven

Pacific
Palisades

1. EDDIE ALBERT/719 Almalfi Dr.
2. JAMES ARNESS/830 Brooktree Rd.
3. CHEVY CHASE/17492 Camino Yatasto
4. BILL COSBY/1500 Sorrento Dr.
5. JOSEPH COTTEN/17800 Tramonto
6. BILLY CRYSTAL/860 Chautauqua Blvd.
7. JOHN GOODMAN/619 Amalfi Dr.
8. GOLDIE HAWN & KURT RUSSEL/1422 Capri Dr.
9. ANTHONY HOPKINS/1331 Monument St.
10. MICHAEL KEATON/812 and 826 Napoli Dr.
11. CHARLES LAUGHTON/14950 Corona del Mar
12. WALTER MATTHAU/278 Toyopa Dr.
13. JENNY McCARTHY/1476 Via Cresta
14. ARNOLD SCHWARZENEGER & MARIA SHRIVER/14209 Sunset Blvd.
15. LAWRENCE WELK/1694 Alta Mura Rd.

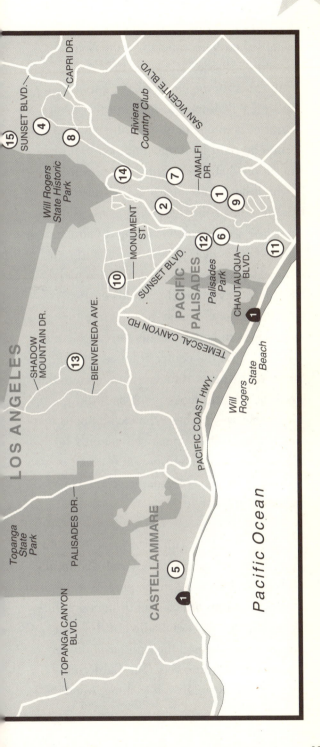

IN THE LATE NINETEENTH CENTURY, the old California land-grant families established their ranches in the sage-covered hillsides known as the Pacific Palisades. In the early 1920s, a fellow named Will Rogers helped put this semi-rural coastal community on the national map when he built his ranch and polo field just north of what is now Sunset Boulevard (which had other names at the time and was nothing but a dusty trail). Rogers, who was not just a Hollywood star, but a national icon vis-à-vis his newspaper column and radio show, loved the Palisades. He also had a home in Beverly Hills, but his early California-style ranch, nestled into the Palisades hillside, was his retreat, his place of work, and the center of his family life. The Will Rogers Ranch is now open to the public and still looks much as it did when its owner was perhaps the most famous man in America. It is a must-see not only for those who love celebrity real estate, but also for the curious seeking a peek into early California lifestyle.

Rogers's ranch was also responsible for the proliferation of what we now call California Ranch architecture. In the post–World War II years, many architects and designers influenced by the style embodied in Rogers's early vision created the California dream home for returning vets. The California Ranch was typically a low-slung, wood-sided, paned-windowed home with a comfortable feeling. In the 1950s and 1960s, the Pacific Palisades would see many ranch-style homes built for the burgeoning population, and the area would in fact be one of the first in the nation to build this style of home. One of the more distinguished of the ranch builders was architect Cliff May, actually credited as the father of California Ranch. May's main turf was the Westside of Los Angeles, with many commissions in the Palisades. Quite a few of them were for celebrity clients, and many still stand today in their original and preserved state.

Throughout the 1950s, 1960s, and 1970s, Pacific Palisades was a quiet family community, avoiding all the flash and sophistication of its neighbors to the east. Stars who lived in the Palisades did so to escape the hullabaloo of the Beverly Hills crowd. One of the most famous of the Palisades families was that of Ronald and Nancy Reagan. The former president and his second wife raised their two children in what was then the perfect American post-war community. The schools were excellent, crime was virtually nonexistent, and the Pacific Ocean beckoned beach lovers.

By the 1980s, the real estate boom and gentrification began to transform the ranchy Palisades into more of a village that might be found in the south of France. Actually, the new and mostly large homes of Mediterranean influence that began rising with great frequency about fifteen years ago are in keeping with the terrain. Many of them are quite exquisite, sending a message of quality and success.

This message became increasingly attractive to young Hollywood, and many stars headed west to the Palisades, forsaking the image of Beverly Hills in favor of the simpler values they believed were asserted by this community. The Palisades is no longer the quiet bedroom community of the postwar years, and certainly Will Rogers would be horrified to see what has happened to his dusty trail now known as Sunset Boulevard. However, the clean air, the proximity to the beach, the charming downtown village, and the gorgeous homes surrounded by lush California vegetation create a wonderful life for the stars and regular folks alike who make Pacific Palisades home.

One very famous American citizen will be joining the Palisades family in the year 2000. President Bill Clinton and first lady Hillary have purchased property on Amalfi Drive off Sunset Boulevard, opting to leave Pennsylvania Avenue and their Arkansas roots behind in favor of a California address for their post-presidential years.

1 Eddie Albert

719 Amalfi Drive
Pacific Palisades, CA 90272

Eddie Albert began his show business career in the 1938 comedy *Brother Rat*. Best known for his TV role as Oliver Douglas on the sitcom *Green Acres* (1965-71), Albert has starred in *The Longest Yard* (1974), *The Heartbreak Kid* (1972), *The Sun Also Rises* (1957), and *Oklahoma!* (1955). Married to actress Margo Albert, their son is leading man Edward Albert.

This traditional home, with eighteen rooms, including six bedrooms as well as a pool, was built in 1933. Today's market value exceeds $2.5 million.

Year Built: 1933
Lot Size: 33,933 sq. ft.
Home Size: 4,818 sq. ft.

2 James Arness

830 Brooktree Road
Pacific Palisades, CA 90272

The tall, rugged star of television's *Gunsmoke* for two decades and brother of actor Peter Graves lived during the 1960s and 1970s at 830 Brooktree Road in the Pacific Palisades. This one-story contemporary home, built in 1949, has a gravel roof and stucco walls. The residence, with its eight rooms, including three bedrooms, would have a value of $950,000 in today's market.

Lot Size: 17,206 sq. ft.
Home Size: 2,148 sq. ft.

Chapter Seven

Chevy Chase 3

17492 Camino de Yatasto
Pacific Palisades, CA 90272

WILD AND FUNNY MAN CHEVY CHASE, STAR OF *National Lampoon's Vacation* (1983) and *Caddyshack* (1980), lived during the 1970s and 1980s behind the gates of the Palisades Highlands, a small community of multimillion-dollar homes tucked into a coastal mountainside. Up a very long road that seems never to end but offers spectacular vistas, the homes are visible from the gates or from a vantage point on a street above the development that climbs up the hillside.

Bill Cosby 4

1500 Sorrento Drive
Pacific Palisades, CA 90272

THE UNSPEAKABLE TRAGEDY OF THE DEATH OF BILL AND Camille Cosby's son flashed their Palisades residence all over TV screens around the world. Fans are familiar with the Tudor-style, two-story home purchased by the much-loved star in 1990 for $2,550,000. The Cosby home has sixteen rooms, including four bedrooms and four baths, and value today is well over $3 million.

HOME SIZE: 4,538 SQ. FT.
TAXES: $31,886.31 PER YEAR

5 Joseph Cotten

17800 Tramonto
Pacific Palisades, CA 90272

FOR CLASSIC MOVIE BUFFS, THIS STAR OF THE LATE Orson Welles's Mercury Theater and many great movies of the Golden Era of motion pictures once lived in this wonderful hillside villa. In his later life, Cotten moved to Palm Springs, California. He was married to actress Patricia Medina, who is alive and well and the author of his recently published memoirs titled *Laid Back in Hollywood*. The couple shared a sprawling Palm Springs Mesa area estate know as White Gables.

6 Billy Crystal

860 Chautauqua Boulevard
Pacific Palisades, CA 90272

IF YOU WATCH THE ANNUAL ACADEMY AWARDS OR ENJOY his many films, including *Mr. Saturday Night* (1992), *City Slickers* (1991), and *When Harry Met Sally* (1989), you may be among the legions of fans who laugh with Billy Crystal. Crystal and his longtime wife, Janice, have owned their 4,347-square-foot Palisades home since 1979, when they purchased it for $435,000. Today the home, which has twelve rooms with four bedrooms and four baths, would be worth more than $3 million.

Chapter Seven

John Goodman 7

**619 Amalfi Drive
Pacific Palisades, CA 90272**

THE SIZABLE TELEVISION AND FILM ACTOR——WHO PLAYED substantial character roles in the Coen brothers' *Barton Fink* and *The Big Lebowski* and rose to prominence as *Roseanne*'s husband—lives in a sizable home on Amalfi Drive in the Palisades. Built in 1946, the thirteen-room, five-bedroom traditional has a pool and a view.

LOT SIZE: *13,634* SQ. FT.
HOME SIZE: *7,806* SQ. FT.
ASSESSED VALUE: *$1,850,900*

Goldie Hawn 8
Kurt Russell

**1422 Capri Drive
Pacific Palisades, CA 90272**

REBUILT IN 1990, THIS MASSIVE CONTEMPORARY RESIdence is held in title under the name Goldie Hawn. It's rumored that Kurt Russell spends a great deal of time at the twelve-room estate on nearly one acre.

Purchased in 1988 for a reported $2,100,000, Hawn's home is today assessed at $4,389,800. Not bad for the *Laugh-In* zany, who went on to star in *Bird on a Wire* (1990), *Overboard* (1987), *Private Benjamin* (1980), *Shampoo* (1975), and the recent box office hit *The First Wives Club*.

LOT SIZE: *35,545* SQ. FT.
HOME SIZE: *12,860* SQ. FT.
TAXES: *$46,754.13* PER YEAR

9 Anthony Hopkins

1331 Monument Street
Pacific Palisades, CA 90272

NOT A KILLER HOUSE FOR THE KILLER BEHIND THE Oscar®-winning movie *The Silence of the Lambs*. Purchased in 1995 at $660,000, this modest home of 1,388 square feet is the perfect three-bedroom, two-bath hideaway for Hopkins. The recent upswing in the market has most probably added 20 percent to the value of Hopkins's Palisades abode.

10 Michael Keaton

812 and 826 Napoli Drive
Pacific Palisades, CA 90272

BORN WITH THE NAME MICHAEL DOUGLAS THIS ACTOR changed his name for obvious reasons and did quite well. The star of *Batman Returns* (1992), *Mr. Mom* (1983), *Night Shift* (1982), *Working Stiffs* (1979), owns a super set of properties on exclusive Napoli Drive. He first bought 826 Napoli on July 10, 1987, and then purchased 812 Napoli in 1988. The first home has sixteen rooms with four bedrooms and four baths, and the second has thirteen rooms in just over 3,584 square feet. Keaton paid more than $1,500,000 for the first and $1,700,000 for the second.

Charles Laughton 11

14950 Corona del Mar
Pacific Palisades, CA 90272

THIS STAR OF THE CLASSIC MOVIES *THE HUNCHBACK OF NOTRE DAME* (1939) and *Mutiny on the Bounty* (1935) must have been inspired by this home on the high cliffs over the Pacific at the edge of the Palisades. What a perfect place for a murder—over the cliff goes the evidence! Corona del Mar is actually one of the most exclusive streets in the Palisades. Many of the homes are valued in the multiple millions. Some, however, are valueless, as their backyard cliffs above the Pacific Ocean and the Coast Highway below have eroded beyond repair.

Walter Matthau 12

278 Toyopa Drive
Pacific Palisades, CA 90272

TIME MAGAZINE SAID WALTER MATTHAU WAS "ABOUT AS likely a candidate for stardom as the neighborhood delicatessen man." But become a star Matthau did—including sexy leading-man roles such as the bank robber–pilot in director Don Siegel's *Charley Varrick* (1973). His straight roles, however, were buried as he gained a reputation for comedy in *The Odd Couple, Hello Dolly!, The Sunshine Boys,* and *Dennis the Menace.* Now ensconced in the Huntington Palisades neighborhood, Matthau lives with his wife, Carol, in a multimillion-dollar home that is not ostentatious but rather formidable, traditional, and substantial-looking. Here the Matthaus occupy sixteen rooms, with five bedrooms and seven baths.

Lot Size: 38,507 sq. ft.
Home Size: 9,828 sq. ft.

13 Jenny McCarthy
1476 Via Cresta
Pacific Palisades, CA 90272

THIS YOUNG, DYNAMIC CENTERFOLD, ACTRESS, AND AUTHOR closed escrow on 1476 Via Cresta in the Palisades in Spring 1998 for a reported purchase price of $2,265,000. The 4,592-square-foot home with a pool was built in 1988 and has three bedrooms and four baths. Sitting on 2.19 acres, the view property is one of the largest lots in the area.

Arnold Schwarzenegger 14
Maria Shriver

14209 Sunset Boulevard
Pacific Palisades, CA 90049

RECENTLY PURCHASING PROPERTY NEXT DOOR, ACTOR-BODY builder Arnold Schwarzenegger, star of *Terminator* and *Terminator 2*, *Total Recall*, *Kindergarten Cop*, and *Twins*, and his journalist wife Maria Shriver have created a multimillion-dollar compound in the tradition of Shriver's Kennedy family roots. The original house at 14209 Sunset rests on a 60,113-square-foot pad. Built in 1982, it contains fifteen bedrooms and baths in 6,496 square feet.

The Schwarzeneggers pay $26,462.50 per year in property tax on this parcel.

Lawrence Welk 15

1694 Alta Mura Road
Pacific Palisades, CA 90272

"AND A-ONE, AND A-TWO,"... CHAMPAGNE MUSIC bandleader, TV star, businessman, and real estate mogul Lawrence Welk loved living by the ocean. His former home at 1694 Alta Mura Road, built in 1966 in contemporary style, is not ostentatious given the wealth amassed by this late American icon.

The one-story, three-bedroom home has a stucco exterior, pool, wood shake roof, and a wonderful view.

LOT SIZE: 43,120 SQ. FT.
HOME SIZE: 4,585 SQ. FT.

Chapter Eight

Santa Monica

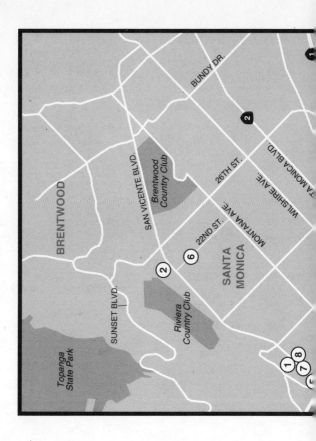

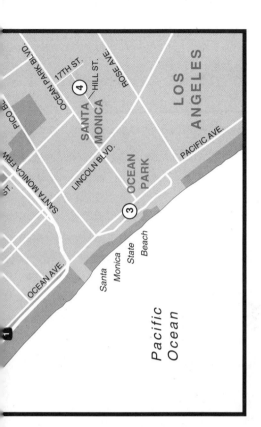

1. JEFF BRIDGES/436 Adelaide Dr.
2. MEL BROOKS & ANNE BANCROFT/2301 La Mesa Dr.
3. JAMIE LEE CURTIS/158 Wadsworth
4. HEATHER GRAHAM/1633 Hill St.
5. LARRY HAGMAN/101 Ocean Ave.
6. DYLAN McDERMOTT/320 22nd St.
7. JEAN SMART/3332 Stoner Ave.
8. SYLVESTER STALLONE/323 San Vicente Blvd.

Like the rest of Los Angeles, the city of Santa Monica, founded in the 1880s by forward-thinking men and women who envisioned a great port for the Los Angeles basin at their doorstep, is a community in transition. Once quiet and conservative (although there were wild times in wild periods in places like Ocean Park and in old hotels and bathhouses that used to line the Pacific oceanfront), Santa Monica by virtue of its politics and its people is a conflicted mix of liberal activism meeting staunch "hold the line" reactionary ideas, set in a Disney-esque American town by the sea.

You can see the old world meeting the new head-on in the architecture of this beachfront city. Artists have colonized certain sectors, and trendy retail and dining have taken over the previously mom-and-pop storefronts of swank Montana Avenue, where a laundromat, bakery, and cafe called Sweet 16 at Montana and 16th Street once offered about the most excitement possible.

Home to many writers, directors, and actors, Santa Monica offers a place to unwind and escape Hollywood without leaving town. Gillette Regent Square is the upper end of this community. A street called La Mesa, which borders the Pacific Rim, running parallel to San Vicente as it winds out of Brentwood into Santa Monica and on to Ocean

SANTA MONICA

Avenue and the beach, is possibly one of the most desirable of all streets on the Westside. It is and has been home to many stars.

Before you head to the beach and out to Malibu, take in the charm of Santa Monica. A stroll along the Palisades Beach Promenade adjacent to Ocean Avenue and the cliffs above the Pacific Coast Highway at Sunset probably will not bring you face-to-face with stars . . . it's a bit too public and busy. However, look over the cliffs at the beach houses (some are mansions) below on the sand fronting Santa Monica. This is known as the Gold Coast, and almost every home you view belonged at one point in time to some of the most famous names in entertainment. Today, most are owned by private families, and the property has changed hands many times. The most magnificent of all the homes unfortunately no longer stands. The beach house of Marion Davies, built by publishing mogul William Randolph Hearst, was the extreme example of West Coast palatial in terms of the Hollywood beach houses. Built in Southern colonial style, the massive 100-plus-room mansion fronting the sand was the ultimate Hollywood playground for several decades. Today only the garage house and guest quarters remain, owned and controlled by the city of Santa Monica, and often used as a site for filming such popular shows as *Beverly Hills, 90210* and *Baywatch*.

Chapter Eight

Jeff Bridges 1

436 Adelaide Drive
Santa Monica, CA 90402

When his young star was on the rise during the 1970s and early 1980s before his migration north to Santa Barbara, Jeff Bridges, star of *Blown Away* (1994), *The Last Picture Show* (1991), and *The Morning After* (1986), lived at 436 Adelaide Drive in Santa Monica.

This stately old Spanish territorial–designed home, dating from the 1920s, stands elegantly against the reflections of the Pacific resting beyond the Santa Monica Canyon hill on which the home sits.

Jeff Bridges, son of Lloyd Bridges, also maintains a home in Malibu. (See Chapter Nine.)

Mel Brooks 2
Anne Bancroft

2301 La Mesa Drive
Santa Monica, CA 90402

Acerbic writer, satirical performer, and producer/director Mel Brooks of *Blazing Saddles* fame lives with renowned Tony Award–winning actress and wife Anne Bancroft—"Mrs. Robinson"—in a dramatic contemporary home based on a French-European theme. The massive copper roof, constructed along the interpreted line of a classic mansard rests on a formidable gray stucco residence with more than 13,000 square feet of living space.

★ 3 Jamie Lee Curtis

**158 Wadsworth
Santa Monica, CA 90402**

DURING THE 1970S IN HER EARLY CAREER, JAMIE LEE Curtis, daughter of actors Tony Curtis and Janet Leigh and star of *True Lies* (1994), *A Fish Called Wanda* (1988), and *Trading Places* (1983), lived in this Santa Monica fourplex building built in 1915. The small, charming older building is in a beach-close locale and has a market value of more than $600,000 today.

Lot Size: 3,511 sq. ft.
Square Feet of Building: 4,422
Home Size: 4 One-Bedroom, One-Bath Apartments
Assessed Value of Curtis's unit: $71,100

★ 4 Heather Graham

**1633 Hill Street
Santa Monica, CA 90405**

ACTRESS HEATHER GRAHAM LIVES WITH HUSBAND KEN at trendy 1633 Hill Street. This artists' colony, a neighborhood in transition, rests in the old beach-and-boardwalk section of Santa Monica, up the hill from the Pacific Ocean.

The couple purchased this small but charm-ing stucco home in 1994 at a reported cost of $315,000.

Lot Size: 7,048 sq. ft.
Home Size: 1,133 sq. ft.
Rooms: 6, with 2 Bedrooms and 1 Bath

Chapter Eight

Larry Hagman 5

101 Ocean Avenue
Los Angeles, CA 90402

DALLAS STAR LARRY HAGMAN AND HIS WIFE OWN AN elegant Santa Monica condo at 101 Ocean Avenue. Unit A features a spacious interior of 3,029 square feet with panoramic Pacific Ocean vistas. Purchased in 1996 for a reported sale price of $1,450,000, the condo has two bedrooms and three baths.

Dylan McDermott 6

320 22nd Street
Santa Monica, CA 90402

THE STAR OF THE HIT TV SERIES *THE PRACTICE* LIVES IN a very quiet residential section of Santa Monica known as Gillette Regent Square. McDermott purchased this home in 1995 for $790,000.

LOT SIZE: **7,549** SQ. FT.
HOME SIZE: **2,130** SQ. FT.

7 Jean Smart

3332 Stoner Avenue
Los Angeles, CA 90066

JEAN SMART IS BEST KNOWN FOR HER LONG-RUNNING success on television's *Designing Women*. Other TV roles include *Scarlett*, a CBS-TV miniseries, "The Yearling," also a CBS-TV movie production, and "Just My Imagination," a NBC telefilm. On screen, Smart has starred in *Guinevere, The Odd Couple II, The Brady Bunch Movie,* and *Mistress.*

This rising star recently bought a three-bedroom Westside bungalow. Built in 1947, it has one story and a garden.

Lot Size: 9.326 sq. ft.
Home Size: 1,469 sq. ft
Purchased by Smart in: 1998
Purchase Price: $417,500

8 Sylvester Stallone

323 San Vicente Boulevard
Santa Monica, CA 90402

THE SUPERSTAR ACTION HERO OF *THE SPECIALIST* (1995), *First Blood* (1982), and *Rocky* (1976), Stallone owns this condo, which features one bedroom and three baths in 1,830 square feet. Stallone reportedly paid $390,000 for the residence in 1985. It has recently been assessed at $486,400.

Chapter Eight

Chapter Nine

Malibu
(East)

1. LAURALEE BELL/23720 Malibu Colony Rd.
2. JEFF BRIDGES/2882 Hume Rd.
3. LLOYD BRIDGES/21540 Pacific Coast Hwy.
4. CHARLES BRONSON/3661 Cross Creek Rd.
5. MEL BROOKS & ANNE BANCROFT/23868 Malibu Rd.
7. DEAN CAIN/3224 Malibu Canyon. Rd.
8. DYAN CANNON/98 Malibu Colony Rd.
10. CHER/27422 Pacific Coast Hwy.
12. JACKIE COLLINS/26829 Malibu Dr.
13. BRUCE DERN/23430 Malibu Colony Dr.
20. KRIS KRISTOFFERSON/3179 Sumac Ridge Rd.
23. SHIRLEY MacLAINE/25200 Old Malibu Rd.
25. OLIVIA NEWTON-JOHN/3655 McAnany Way
29. BURT REYNOLDS/22336 Pacific Coast Hwy.
36. GEORGE WENDT/23458 W. Moon Shadows Dr.

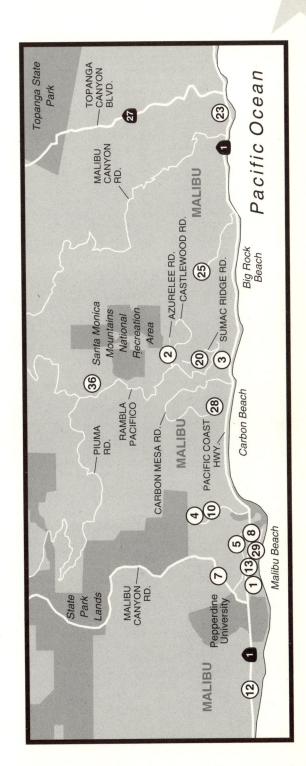

147

Chapter Nine

Malibu (West)

6. NICOLAS CAGE/33014 Pacific Coast Hwy.
9. JOHNNY CARSON/6915 Whitesand Pl.
11. DAVID CHARVET/3551 Cross Creek Rd.
14. ROBERT DUVALL/6238 Bonsall Dr.
15. BOB DYLAN/29400 Bluewater
16. LOUIS GOSSETT JR./6614 Dume Dr.
17. GOLDIE HAWN/30804 Broadbeach Rd.
18. MICHAEL JACKSON/6982 Wildlife Rd.
19. JACK KLUGMAN/22548 Pacific Coast Hwy.
21. TOMMY LEE • PAMELA ANDERSON/31341 Mulholland Hwy.
22. ALI MacGRAW/1108 Broadbeach Rd.
24. WALTER MATTHAU/30936 Broadbeach Rd.
26. JACK NICHOLSON/5020 Yerba Buena
27. NICK NOLTE/6153 & 6173 Bonsall Dr. & 29555 Rainsford Pl.
28. SEAN PENN/22271 Carbon Mesa Rd.
30. LINDA RONSTADT/38 Malibu Colony Rd.
31. MARTIN SHEEN/6916 Dume Dr.
32. FRANK SINATRA/30966 Broadbeach Rd.
33. AARON SPELLING/21536 Pacific Coast Hwy.
34. SYLVESTER STALLONE/30900 Broadbeach Rd.
35. BARBRA STREISAND/5750 Ramirez Cyn.
37. BRUCE WILLIS/22470 Pacific Coast Hwy.

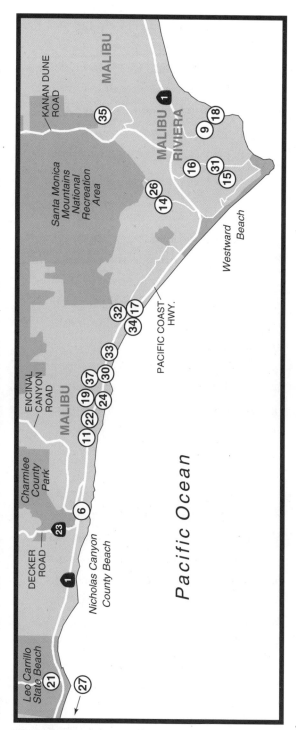

WHEN ONE THINKS OF MALIBU, that rustic and romantic slice of the California coast, one can't help but wonder: Is it really worth fighting the ravages of nature—from fires and floods to landslides and earthquakes—in order to live there? Malibu, by virtue of nature's anger and the unyielding affinity of celebrity property owners, has become famous the world over.

It is the beach town of the stars. And a place called the Colony, just off the Pacific Coast Highway in the center of the town of Malibu, is the place to be and be seen. The Colony is a virtual who's who of Hollywood. It has been thus for decades, and it continues to change as celebrities buy and sell, rise and fall, move east and south and then back again, tire of the ravages of nature and then miss them, seeking to return. The title reports on Colony properties list dozens of stars as owners then and now.

Such is the record for much of the rest of Malibu, or The Malibu as old-timers and purists call this area of rugged California beauty. Homes hug the rim of the highway fronting the ocean, all up and down the Malibu coast. Some are worth multiple millions, others are ramshackle but still valued at close to a million dollars for their coveted location. In the hills and valleys above the coast, ranches such as Barbra Streisand's compound, recently on the market at some $25 million before the superstar chose to donate the property and make it a preserve, are mixed with cabins and smaller homes.

Malibu is a mysterious place that gets in your blood, say some longtime aficionados. Perhaps it will do the same for you as you check out the beach homes of your favorite stars. In many cases, all you will be able to see is the garage fronting the highway. And the Colony gate is the closest you'll get to the beachfront row of star homes. That is, unless Johnny Carson invites you over for a drink and maybe a game of tennis.

Lauralee Bell 1

23720 Malibu Colony Road
Malibu, CA 90265

HER PERSONAL SUCCESS AS A CO-STAR OF *THE YOUNG and the Restless*, and her family pedigree enable this young star to afford the luxury of a substantial Malibu retreat. Bell purchased the home in 1990 for a reported $3,500,000. Built in 1983, the English-style, ten-room, two-story beach house sits on a 26 x 300–foot sand lot comprising 7,797 square feet of precious land.

TAXES: $35,080.82 PER YEAR

Jeff Bridges 2

2882 Hume Road
Malibu, CA 90265

THIS SUPERSTAR AND SANTA BARBARA RESIDENT also owns 2882 Hume Road in Malibu. This two-story home, with three bedrooms and three baths, was built in 1951, damaged by fire, and rebuilt.

Owned by Bridges and his family for many years, this property has not been recently assessed. Its value today probably would be close to $1 million.

LOT SIZE: 35,275 SQ. FT.
HOME SIZE: 1,608 SQ. FT.

3 Lloyd Bridges

21540 Pacific Coast Highway
Malibu, CA 90265

THE LATE ACTOR, HIS WIFE DOROTHY, AND THE FAMILY have lived at and loved their beach house since 1959, when Bridges bought 21540 Pacific Coast Highway. This beachfront home has been the site of countless family gatherings. Its market value exceeds $2.5 million.

LOT SIZE: 5,171 SQ. FT.
HOME SIZE: 2,412 SQ. FT.
ROOMS: 9, WITH 4 BEDROOMS AND 3 BATHS

4 Charles Bronson

3661 Cross Creek Road
Malibu, CA 90265

THIS RUGGED STAR OF ACTION FILMS IN THE 1960s AND 1970s set the tone for his successors: Arnold Schwarzenegger, Chuck Norris, Steven Seagal, and Bruce Willis. Bronson and his late wife, actress Jill Ireland, lived in many locations from Beverly Hills to Brentwood to Malibu. One of the early Bronson homes, which he purchased in 1962, is located at 3661 Cross Creek Road. Built in 1947, this two-bedroom, two-bath home on a large parcel of land was, and remains, a wonderful retreat.

LOT SIZE: 3.92 ACRES
HOME SIZE: 1,871 SQ. FT.
TAXES: $9,310.65 PER YEAR

Chapter Nine

Mel Brooks 5
Anne Bancroft

23868 Malibu Road
Malibu, CA 90265

Built in 1927, this traditional home with more than 3,000 feet on Malibu Road is the beach house of Mel Brooks and Anne Bancroft.

Purchased in 1977 before the property gold rush, Brooks paid a substantial $515,000 for the property, which today would be worth perhaps $5 million.

Lot Size: **14,972 sq. ft.**
Home Size: **3,476 sq. ft.**
Taxes: **$10,418.92 per year**

Nicolas Cage 6

33014 Pacific Coast Highway
Malibu, CA 90265

Beverly Hills High graduate Nicolas Cage, Oscar®-winning star of *Leaving Las Vegas* (1996), *Snake Eyes* (1998), *Face/Off* (1997), and *Raising Arizona* (1987), owned this Pacific Coast Highway getaway. Purch-ased in 1997 for a reported $3,300,000, the house has two bedrooms and three baths.

Lot Size: **38,184 sq. ft.**
Home Size: **2,810 sq. ft.**
Taxes: **$33,212.92 per year**

MALIBU

7 Dean Cain
3224 Malibu Canyon Road
Malibu, CA 90265

"SUPERMAN" LIVES IN THIS ONE-STORY HOME BUILT IN 1957 with a wonderful view. The star of *Lois and Clark: The New Adventures of Superman* and co-star of *Future Sport* purchased his two-bedroom Malibu residence in 1997. The market value today is more than $500,000.

LOT SIZE: **25,692** *SQ. FT.*
HOME SIZE: **1,767** *SQ. FT.*

8 Dyan Cannon
98 Malibu Colony Road
Malibu, CA 90265

THREE-TIME OSCAR®-NOMINATED ACTRESS AND FILMMAKER Dyan Cannon can often be seen on Fox's *Ally McBeal*. The former wife of the late Cary Grant and mother of his child, Jennifer Grant, an aspiring actress, lives the good life in the Malibu Colony.

Her beach house, photographed and featured in *Architectural Digest* and other stylish publications, is a waterfront, contemporary Southwest paradise furnished in white, overstuffed, canvas-duck upholstered furniture.

Star of *The Rise and Fall of Legs Diamond* (1960), *Author! Author!* (1982), and 1978's *Heaven Can Wait*, Cannon is often spotted shopping in the Malibu Country Mart across the Coast Highway from the Colony.

Chapter Nine

Johnny Carson 9

6915 Whitesand Place
Malibu, CA 90265

LONGTIME *TONIGHT SHOW* HOST JOHNNY CARSON OWNS multiple properties in Malibu. They include 6915 Whitesand Place and 6962 Wildlife Road. The former home was built in 1988 on more than one acre of land and has 2,751 square feet, and two bedrooms. Assessed in 1998 at $2,103,400, the property has a tax bill of $22,694.12 per year.

The latter residence is a beach house with a pool, built in 1980. It features 7,083 square feet on approximately one acre of land. This two-bedroom, four-bath home is assessed at $6,921,900 and comes with an annual tax bill of $74,135.13.

David Charvet 11

3551 Cross Creek Road
Malibu, CA 90265

BORN IN LYON, FRANCE, DAVID FRANK CHARVET MOVED to America at age eight with his mother, Christiane. As a young man working in a retail shop, David was noticed by a photographer who introduced him to the world of modeling. His career took off immediately, and sponsors such as Levi's and Coca-Cola placed Charvet in national ad campaigns.

Acting was a natural expansion of David's modeling career, and drama school led him to small roles and the eventual casting as Matt on the enormously successful television show *Baywatch*.

Charvet portrayed Matt from 1992 until 1995, leaving the show to pursue other opportunities, including a role on *Melrose Place*.

Charvet purchased this four-bedroom place on Cross Creek Road in spring 1998 for a reported figure of $1,275,000.

YEAR BUILT: 1961
HOME SIZE: 2,726 SQ. FT.

10 Cher
27422 Pacific Coast Hwy
Malibu, CA 90265

OSCAR®-WINNING ACTRESS AND SINGER, CHER buys and sells property as if she were in the real estate business. This three-bedroom beachfront condo with a pool is one of her former residences, quite visible from the highway.

CURRENT TAXES: $8,568 PER YEAR.

Chapter Nine

Jackie Collins 12

26829 Malibu Drive
Malibu, CA 90265

> She's the prolific writer of bestselling glamour fiction: *Hollywood Wives*, *Lucky*, *Chances*, *Rock Star*, and *Hollywood Husbands* to name a few. The ocean views from her Malibu Drive home no doubt inspire some of her best love scenes.

Bruce Dern 13

23430 Malibu Colony Drive
Malibu, CA 90265

> Bruce Dern, father of Laura and co-star of *Diggstown* (1992), *Silent Running* (1972), and *The Great Gatsby* (1974), and his wife, Angie, share a two-story Malibu Colony home by the sea with two fireplaces, wood floors, and many handsome features including an ocean-view deck. Built in 1928, the six-bedroom estate sits on a 5,650-square-foot beach lot assessed at $647,806. The market value of the residence is over $4 million.

14 Robert Duvall

6238 Bonsall Drive
Malibu, CA 90265

NOMINATED FOR AN OSCAR® FOR HIS FILM *The Apostle* (1997), Robert Duvall is a man for all seasons, an actor's actor whose credits include *Days of Thunder* (1990), *Apocalypse Now* (1979), *The Godfather* (1972), and *Tender Mercies* (1983) for which he won an Oscar®.

During the 1980s Duvall lived in Malibu at 6238 Bonsall Drive in this one-story, two-bedroom contemporary home built in 1951. The property was transferred to the present owner in 1995 for a reported sale price of $1,480,500.

LOT SIZE: 3.8 ACRES
HOME SIZE: 4,251 SQ. FT.

15 Bob Dylan

29400 Bluewater
Malibu, CA 90265

ROCKER-POET BOB DYLAN (FATHER OF JAKOB) OWNS A two-bedroom Malibu pad, built in 1948, which he purchased in 1984. The value of this residence exceeds $1 million.

Chapter Nine

Louis Gossett Jr. 16

6614 Dume Drive
Malibu, CA 90265

STAR OF *A RAISIN IN THE SUN* ON BOTH STAGE AND film, Louis Gossett Jr., the talented actor from Brooklyn, New York, starred in such films as *An Officer and a Gentleman* (1986) and the acclaimed TV miniseries *Roots*. His 1980s Malibu home at 6614 Dume Drive is a one-story contemporary house with four bedrooms and three baths, built in 1953.

LOT SIZE: 2 ACRES
TAXES: $5,068.16 PER YEAR

Goldie Hawn 17

30804 Broadbeach Road
Malibu, CA 90265

GOLDIE HAWN, WHO RECENTLY MADE AUDIENCES LAUGH in *The First Wives Club*, owns a wonderful coastal retreat on Broadbeach Road in Malibu.

This two-story, four bedroom home, built in 1978 and contemporary in style, features nearly 4,000 feet. Market value today would be double the assessed value below.

LOT SIZE: 15,560 SQ. FT.
ASSESSED VALUE: $2,176,000
TAXES: $23,399.03 PER YEAR

18 Michael Jackson

6982 Wildlife Road
Malibu, CA 90265

THE INTERNATIONAL MEGA-PERFORMER SPENDS MOST OF his time on his ranch in the Santa Ynez Valley, north of Santa Barbara. Jackson and his family have owned many properties all over the Los Angeles region, from their childhood home on Hayvenhurst Avenue in Encino to this 1980s Malibu retreat with eight rooms, including two bedrooms, at 6982 Wildlife Road.

Lot Size: 43,996 sq. ft.
Home Size: 1997 sq. ft.
Sale Date: 9/9/94
Sale Amount: $2,000,000
Assessed Value: $2,062,643
Taxes: $22,295.96 per year

19 Jack Klugman

22548 Pacific Coast Highway
Malibu, CA 90265

THIS WELL-RESPECTED ACTOR ONCE OWNED THIS ONE-bedroom condo on the ocean in Malibu. Almost 1,600 square feet in a building built in 1963 on the coast was a welcome retreat for the much in-demand actor, best known for his role in *The Odd Couple* TV series opposite Tony Randall. Today the condo's market value is over $350,000.

Chapter Nine

Kris Kristofferson 20

3179 Sumac Ridge Road
Malibu, CA 90265

PURCHASED IN 1974 FOR A REPORTED $165,000, THIS Malibu home with nine rooms, including three bedrooms, was built in 1948 and has a pool. Its market value today would exceed $1 million. A singer, songwriter, and actor, the multitalented Kristofferson is known for his roles in *A Star Is Born* (1976) and *Alice Doesn't Live Here Anymore* (1974).

LOT SIZE: **40,368** SQ. FT.
HOME SIZE: **2,610** SQ. FT.

Tommy Lee 21
Pamela Anderson

31341 Mulholland Highway
Malibu, CA 90265

THEY'VE SPLIT, BUT THE SIX-BEDROOM HOUSE AT 31341 Mulholland Highway in Malibu, high atop the Santa Monica Mountains, is still in both of their celebrity names.

Built in 1991, the home was purchased by Lee and Anderson in 1996 for over $1 million.

LOT SIZE: **2 ACRES**
HOME SIZE: **7,462** SQ. FT.

22 Ali MacGraw
1108 Broadbeach Road
Malibu, CA 90265

THE GIRL FROM SWANK POUND RIDGE, NEW YORK, WHO was married to Steve McQueen and Robert Evans and starred in such films as *The Getaway* (1972), and *Love Story* (1970), and *Goodbye Columbus* (1969), owns a serene coastal home on celebrity-popular Broadbeach Road, considered by many Malibu aficionados to be the best stretch of sand on the Southern California coast.

23 Shirley MacLaine
25200 Old Malibu Road
Malibu, CA 90265

SHIRLEY MACLAINE, WARREN BEATTY'S TALENTED SISTER, bestselling author, and star of *Sweet Charity* (1969), *Irma La Douce* (1963), *Ocean's Eleven* (1960), *The Apartment* (1960), *Around the World in 80 Days* (1956), *Guarding Tess* (1994), and *Terms of Endearment* (1983), owned a beach-front condo at 25200 Malibu Road during the 1970s and 1980s.

The eight-unit building on the sand is valued in the millions. Built in 1963, the units have two or three bedrooms and two baths, and measure approximately 1,200 to 2,000 square feet each, with panoramic Pacific vistas.

Chapter Nine

Walter Matthau 24

30936 Broadbeach Road
Malibu, CA 90265

A BEACH HOUSE FOR FUNNY MAN WALTER MATTHAU and his wife, Carol, rests at 30936 Broadbeach Road in Malibu. Their main residence is located in the Pacific Palisades (see Chapter Seven).

Built in 1963, and reportedly purchased by Matthau in 1987, this large, 4,165-square-foot home with an ocean view has five bedrooms and four baths. Today's market value of this house exceeds $3 million.

Olivia Newton-John 25

3655 McAnany Way
Malibu, CA 90265

SHE LIT UP THE SCREEN IN *GREASE* AND CONTINUES TO delight audiences worldwide. Olivia Newton-John enjoyed life in Malibu for many years. One of her former homes was at 3655 McAnany Way in the hills above the coast. Here she kept her garden and her animals in a five-bedroom country-style home built in 1958.

LOT SIZE: **3.06** *ACRES*
HOME SIZE: **5,964** *SQ. FT.*

MALIBU

26 Jack Nicholson

5020 Yerba Buena
Malibu, CA 90265

When he's not at home on Mulholland Drive (see Chapter Three) or in his front-and-center seats at the Forum for the L.A. Lakers games, Jack Nicholson, actor, director, writer, and producer with credits that include *A Few Good Men* (1992), *Batman* (1989), *Prizzi's Honor* (1985), *Reds* (1981), *Terms of Endearment* (1983), *The Shining* (1980), *Five Easy Pieces* (1970), *One Flew Over the Cuckoo's Nest* (1975), and *Easy Rider* (1969), might be "hangin' out" in Malibu.

Nick Nolte 27

6153 Bonsall Drive
Malibu, CA 90265

Nick Nolte, star of *The Prince of Tides* (1991), *Cape Fear* (1991), *Down and Out in Beverly Hills* (1986), and *The Deep* (1977), is the proud owner of three properties in Malibu, comprising five acres.

29555 Rainsford Place
Malibu, CA 90265
Lot Size: 2 Acres
Home Size: 1,662 sq. ft.
Rooms: 9, with 3 Bedrooms, 2 Baths
Purchased by Nolte in: 1995

6153 Bonsall Drive
Malibu, CA 90265
Lot Size: 1 Acre
Home Size: 4,095 sq. ft.
Rooms: 15, with 3 Bedrooms and 4 Baths
Purchased by Nolte in: 1995
Assessed Value: $1,652,000

6173 Bonsall Drive
Malibu, CA 90265
Home Size: 1,662 sq. ft.
Rooms: 4 bedrooms, 4 baths
Purchased by Nolte in: 1995

Chapter Nine

Sean Penn 28

22271 Carbon Mesa Road
Malibu, CA 90265

REBEL AND OSCAR®-NOMINATED ACTOR SEAN PENN, former husband of Madonna and co-star of *Taps* (1981), *Bad Boys* (1983), *Dead Man Walking* (1995), and *At Close Range* (1989), owns this Spanish-style home with a tile roof on Carbon Mesa Road.

Built in 1949, this four-bedroom home has a pool and more than 5,000 square feet of living space. Given the acreage of this estate, its market value today would be more than $10 million, depending on the divisibility of its fourteen-acre parcel.

29 Burt Reynolds

22336 Pacific Coast Highway
Malibu, CA 90265

BURT REYNOLDS, THE *DELIVERANCE* (1972) STAR WHO made it big with films such as *Rough Cut* (1980), *Smokey and the Bandit* (1977), and *The Longest Yard* (1974), has lived in many Westside homes, with various wives, over many years.

His former beach house in Malibu, at 22336 Pacific Coast Highway, was sold to the present owner in 1997 at a reported figure of $2,550,000.

This single-family home with a pool was built in 1957, with two stories, two bedrooms, and a gorgeous view.

Architecturally contemporary, with stucco exterior and a composition shingle roof, the home is in the Rancho Topanga section of Malibu, on the coast.

LOT SIZE: 10,890 SQ. FT.
HOME SIZE: 2,862 SQ. FT.

Linda Ronstadt 30

38 Malibu Colony Road
Malibu, CA 90265

THE SULTRY SINGER, WHO ALTERNATES SINGING BETWEEN standards, rock 'n' roll, country western and more, is another celebrity resident of the famous Malibu Colony. Ronstadt's beach house, on a narrow strip of golden California sand, is worth in excess of $4 million.

Chapter Nine

Martin Sheen 31

6916 Dume Drive
Malibu, CA 90265

BORN RAMON ESTEVEZ, A NAME USED BY ONE OF HIS talented sons following in his thespian footsteps, actor Martin Sheen has been a longtime Malibu resident.

The respected actor started on Broadway with a part in *The Subject Was Roses* and went on to star in *Gandhi* (1982), *Apocalypse Now* (1979), and *The Missiles of October* (1974).

Together with his wife, three sons, and daughter, Sheen has lived for some time in this quiet, rustic Dume Drive residence built in 1969 with 2,393 square feet, facing the Pacific.

Frank Sinatra 32

30966 Broadbeach Road
Malibu, CA 90265

FRANK SINATRA'S BEACH HOUSE AT 30966 BROADBEACH Road goes to his fourth wife, Barbara Marx-Sinatra.

Built in 1959 on nearly one-third of an acre, the five-bedroom, five-bath, two-story home sits on a long, narrow beach lot measuring 40 x 370 feet.

Purchased in 1990 for a reported $3,300,000, the annual tax bill comes to $56,211.48.

⭐ 33 Aaron Spelling

21536 Pacific Coast Highway
Malibu, CA 90265

TAX AND TITLE RECORDS SHOW THAT MEGA-PRODUCER Aaron Spelling owns two beach houses on the Pacific Coast Highway. The first, located at 21536 Pacific Coast Highway, was built in 1958 on a 6,700-square-foot lot. The house, visible from the highway, has ten rooms, including three bedrooms and four baths in 3,836 square feet.

The second home is located at 21532 Pacific Coast Highway. This house, built in 1950, has three bedrooms and two baths in 2,401 square feet on a lot measuring 6,277 square feet.

Each property is worth more than $2 million.

⭐ 34 Sylvester Stallone

30900 Broadbeach Road
Malibu, CA 90265

PURCHASED IN 1995, "SLY" HAS A CONTEMPORARY-STYLE beach house built in 1981 on popular Broadbeach Road. The tiled-roof house has sixteen rooms, including three bedrooms as well as a beachside pool.

LOT SIZE: 15,782 SQ. FT.
HOME SIZE: 4,230 SQ. FT.
ROOMS: 16, WITH 3 BEDROOMS, 5 BATHS
TAXES: $31,110.36 PER YEAR

Chapter Nine

Barbra Streisand 35

5750 Ramirez Canyon
Malibu, CA 90265

THE WORLD-CLASS ACTRESS, SINGER, DIRECTOR, AND STAR of *The Mirror Has Two Faces, The Prince of Tides, Yentl* (1983), *Funny Girl* (1968), and *Hello Dolly!* (1969), was a longtime resident of Holmby Hills on exclusive Carolwood Drive, north of Sunset Boulevard. Her estate, near the former mansion of the late Fanny Brice, whom Streisand portrayed in *Funny Girl,* was recently sold for a reported $8 million.

A lover of homes, art, and design, Streisand has also maintained a number of beach homes in Malibu, including this compound on Ramirez Canyon Road. On the market at more than $20 million for some time, Streisand recently gave the property to the Santa Monica Mountains Conservancy, who will preserve the multihouse compound as a park and learning center.

Recently, Streisand married beau James Brolin at another of ther Malibu homes, a mansion in the waterfront off Zumirez Canyon Road.

36 George Wendt

23458 West Moon Shadows Drive
Malibu, CA 90265

THE TV COMIC FROM THE SERIES *CHEERS* OWNS PROPERTY all over the L.A. region, including this four-bedroom home built in 1985. Purchased in 1986 at a reported price of

$389,000, the contemporary residence has a beautiful yard and a view.

Lot Size: 17,799 sq. ft.
Home Size: 3,603 sq. ft.

37 Bruce Willis

22470 Pacific Coast Highway
Malibu, CA 90265

BRUCE WILLIS BOUGHT THIS 1948 VINTAGE BEACH HOUSE on the Pacific Coast Highway. Purchased in 1987 for a reported $2,150,000, the residence has five bedrooms and a pool.

Lot Size: 14,375 sq. ft.
Home Size: 4,847 sq. ft.
Taxes: $27,914.75

Chapter Nine

Chapter Ten

San Fernando Valley (East)

1. RICHARD CRENNA/3951 Valley Meadow Rd.
2. ERIK ESTRADA/3768 Eureka Dr.
3. CLARK GABLE/4535 North Petit Ave.
4. ANDY GARCIA/4323 Forman Ave.
5. JENNIE GARTH/13555 Contour Dr.
6. CUBA GOODING, JR./3200 Coldwater Canyon Ave.
8. BOB HOPE/10436 Moorpark St.
9. RODDY McDOWALL/3110 Brookdale Rd.
11. CYBILL SHEPHERD/16037 Royal Oak Rd.
12. PATRICK SWAYZE/14960 Dickens St. & 11420 Lemoncrest Ave.
13. TIFFANI-AMBER THIESSEN/3523 Wrightwood Court & 4227 Greenbush Ave.
14. JOHN TRAVOLTA/4811 Woodley Ave.
15. ALEX TREBEK/3355 Fryman Rd.
16. DENZEL WASHINGTON/4701 Sancola Ave.

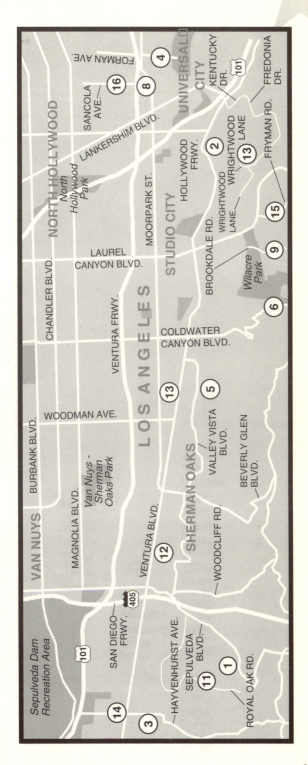

Chapter Ten

San Fernando Valley (West)

7. DAVID HASSELHOFF / 5180 Louise Ave.
10. JOHN RATZENBERGER / 4520 Park Arroyo

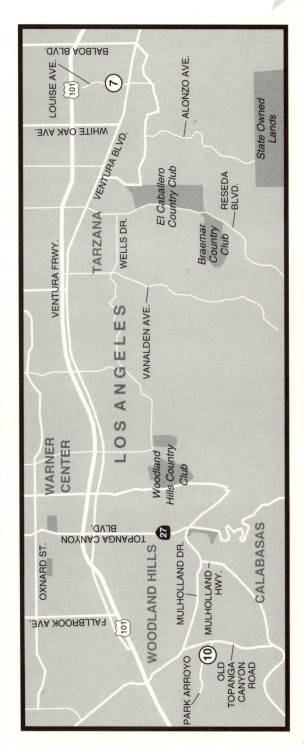

Beverly Hills and Bel Air

may come to mind first when thinking about celebrity homes. However, the vast San Fernando Valley, once a gorgeous expanse of farmland, ranches, and citrus groves, also plays a major role in the Hollywood lifestyle.

Countless stars of early cinema made the Valley home. Many moved over the years as urbanization encroached on their idyllic privacy. Some stayed and remain today, such as the man for all seasons of entertainment, Bob Hope. Lucille Ball and Desi Arnaz had a ranch in Chatsworth, a section of the north Valley, and Clark Gable had major property in Encino, a tony town on the opposite side of the Santa Monica Mountains from Brentwood. In fact, a great portion of the Valley has been developed on celebrity-owned property that once was private, semirural, and reached only by two-lane roads that climbed over the hills from the city.

The end of World War II changed all of that. Vets needed affordable housing, and the Valley was the answer. Even still, freeways did not reach this territory until 1960, when both the San Diego and the Hollywood Freeways opened up the area to that great lifestyle that became known as commuterism.

Today the Valley is a patchwork of neighborhoods and communities of all colors, religions, and cultural, social, and financial backgrounds. From area to area, street to street, even house to house, the San Fernando Valley is the quintessential American landscape of the 1990s. Here are some of the stars, past and present, who love to live in the Valley.

Richard Crenna 1

3951 Valley Meadow Road
Encino, CA 91436

> A SUBSTANTIAL ENCINO ESTATE BUILT IN 1951 FOR A substantial Hollywood actor. From *The Real McCoys* of the 1960s to numerous film and TV projects, Richard Crenna and his wife, Penni, enjoy a six-bedroom contemporary home with pool. The estate is worth more than $1 million in today's market.

LOT SIZE: **50,264 SQ. FT.**
HOME SIZE: **6,300 SQ. FT.**

Erik Estrada 2

3768 Eureka Drive
Studio City, CA 91604

> HE'S THE HUNK WHO ROSE TO NATIONAL FAME ON THE back of a California Highway Patrol "chopper" in the long-running TV series *CHiPs*, Estrada's handsome home has two bedrooms, a view, a garden, and a pool.

YEAR BUILT: **1947**
LOT SIZE: **20,469 SQ. FT.**
HOME SIZE: **2,491 SQ. FT.**

3 Clark Gable
4535 North Petit Avenue
Encino, CA 91316

CLARK GABLE, WHOSE LARGER-THAN-LIFE PORTRAYAL OF Rhett Butler in *Gone With the Wind* (1939) left female fans swooning, was one of Hollywood's biggest stars of the 1930s, 1940s, and 1950s. His other film credits include *Mogambo* (1953), *It Happened One Night* (1934), *Red Dust* (1932), and *Possessed* (1931). His last performance, in *The Misfits* with Marilyn Monroe, was released after his death.

Like many stars of the era, Gable owned property in many parts of Los Angeles. During the golden era of Hollywood he had a vast ranch in the foothills of Encino, south of Ventura Boulevard on the Valley side of the Santa Monica Mountains.

Gable had groves of citrus, horses, and a wonderful ranch house. In the 1980s the property was sold, subdivided, and turned into expensive suburban housing called—what else—but, the Clark Gable Estates.

Gable's final main residence was with his last wife, Kay Sprekels (of the sugar family fortune), at the northeast corner of Roxbury Drive and Sunset Boulevard in Beverly Hills. The one-story California traditional home still stands, although remodeled and updated, and appears much as it did when Gable was in residence.

Andy Garcia 4

4323 Forman Avenue
Toluca Lake, CA 91602

CUBAN-BORN ACTOR ANDRES GARCIA, BETTER KNOWN AS Andy, star of *When a Man Loves a Woman* (1994), *Dead Again* (1991), *Black Rain* (1989), and *The Untouchables* (1987), lives in a formidable older mansion in Toluca Lake, a smart village of upscale residences sandwiched between the movie studios in Burbank and the suburbs of the San Fernando Valley. Built in 1937, this two-story, seven-bedroom traditional home has a pool, large garden, and a wood shake roof. Garcia purchased it in 1993 for a reported $2,260,000.

LOT SIZE: **28,096** sq. ft.
HOME SIZE: **6,747** sq. ft.

Jennie Garth 5

13555 Contour Drive
Van Nuys, CA 91423

THIS POPULAR YOUNG STAR OF TV'S *BEVERLY HILLS, 90210* purchased this valley home in 1991 for a reported sale price of $350,000. Built in 1953, this stucco home has two bedrooms and one bath.

LOT SIZE: **6,199** sq. ft.
HOME SIZE: **1,315** sq. ft.

6 Cuba Gooding Jr.

3200 Coldwater Canyon Boulevard
Studio City, CA 91604

"SHOW ME THE MONEY" MADE MR. GOODING FAMOUS in the Tom Cruise film *Jerry Maguire,* based on the life of a sports agent and his football player client, played by Gooding. The actor makes his home in a 1955-era, two-story traditional estate with four bedrooms and a pool, which he purchased in 1994.

LOT SIZE: 1 ACRE
HOME SIZE: 2,875 SQ. FT.

7 David Hasselhoff

5180 Louise Avenue
Encino, CA 91316

BAYWATCH HUNK DAVID HASSELHOFF LIVES INLAND IN this sprawling five-bedroom Encino estate.

HOME SIZE: 6,148 SQ. FT.
ROOMS: 5 BEDROOMS AND 5 BATHS
PURCHASED BY HASSELHOFF IN: 1996
PURCHASE PRICE: $1,980,000
TAXES: $21,603.94 PER YEAR

SAN FERNANDO VALLEY

Bob Hope 8

10436 Moorpark Street
North Hollywood, CA 91602

THIS LEGENDARY ENTERTAINER, NOW IN HIS NINETIES, and his wife, Dolores, have made this Moorpark Street home their main residence for some fifty-plus years. In addition to his Hollywood career, Hope has business interests in oil, real estate, and sports.

Built in 1939, the traditional English-style two-story home, which is visible from the street, has thirty-four rooms, including eight bedrooms as well as a pool. The Hopes own multiple adjacent properties, making their residence a major compound. The market value of the entire estate would exceed $8 million.

LOT SIZE: 2 ACRES
HOME SIZE: 14,876 SQ. FT.
ROOMS: 34, WITH 8 BEDROOMS, 11 BATHS
ASSESSED VALUE: $749;700
TAXES: $8,776.95 PER YEAR

9 Roddy McDowall

3110 Brookdale Road
Studio City, CA 91604

CHILD STAR AND RESPECTED PHOTOGRAPHER RODDY McDowall, best buddy of Elizabeth Taylor, lived in Studio City in a 1952-era home with twenty-three rooms, including seven bedrooms as well as a pool. McDowall was fourteen when he starred in *Lassie Come Home* (1942), and as an adult his film roles include *The Longest Day* (1962) and *Planet of the Apes* (1968).

LOT SIZE: 17,276 SQ. FT.
HOME SIZE: 5,032 SQ. FT.

10 John Ratzenberger

4520 Park Arroyo
Calabasas, CA 91302

THE COMEDIC ACTOR AND HIS WIFE BOUGHT THIS HOME in the West Valley, where the oak trees climb to much cleaner skies, in 1995 for $355,000. Calabasas, with its good schools, is a family community with newer homes perched on California's rolling hillsides. The Ratzenberger home is a three-bedroom condo with more than 2,000 feet on a standard lot.

LOT SIZE: 6,571 SQ. FT.
HOME SIZE: 2,416 SQ. FT.

SAN FERNANDO VALLEY

Cybill Shepherd 11

16037 Royal Oak Road
Encino, CA 91316

> She's blond. She's beautiful. She's brash. She's the star of TV's *Cybill*. Her movies include *Alice* (1990), *The Heartbreak Kid* (1972), and *The Last Picture Show* (1971), but television has made her a household name. Cybill Shepherd lived during the 1980s in this large and charming traditional estate with twenty-two rooms, including five bedrooms.

Lot Size: **43,560 sq. ft.**
Home Size: **5,352 sq. ft.**

Patrick Swayze 12

14960 Dickens Street
Sherman Oaks, CA 91403
and
11420 Lemoncrest Avenue
Sylmar, CA 91342

> An in-town condo for late nights at the studio, and a ranch house with four acres for horses in Sylmar suits Patrick and his wife, actress/dancer Lisa Niemi Swayze. The star of *Ghost* (1991), *Road House* (1989), and *Dirty Dancing* (1986) built the 15,000-square-foot condo on a pretty Sherman Oaks street south of Ventura Boulevard, with two bedrooms and three baths in 1991 for $290,000.

The ranch house, built in 1948 with four bedrooms and a pool on four acres of land, was purchased in 1984 for $250,000.

Home Size (Ranch House): 3,011 sq. ft.
Sale Date: 9/14/84
Sale Amount: $250,000

13 Tiffani-Amber Thiessen

3523 Wrightwood Court
North Hollywood, CA 91604
and
4227 Greenbush Avenue
Los Angeles, CA 91423

THIS LONG BEACH, CALIFORNIA, GIRL BECAME MISS JUNIOR America in 1987 and later won *Teen Magazine*'s "Great Model Search." First Tiffani-Amber rose to TV fame as Kelly Kapowski on the popular sitcom *Saved by the Bell* (1984-94). Presently, she plays Valerie Malone on *Beverly Hills, 90210.*

Other credits include the telefilms *A Killer Among Friends, The Stranger Beside Me* (1995), and *Buried Secrets* (1996).

The home on Wrightwood was purchased in 1995 for a reported $875,000. The property on Greenbush has been owned by Thiessen since 1993, when it sold at a reported price of $266,000.

Chapter Ten

John Travolta 14

4810 Woodley Avenue
Encino, CA 91316

JOHN TRAVOLTA, STAR OF *PRIMARY COLORS* (1998), *Face/Off* (1997), *Get Shorty* (1995), and *Saturday Night Fever* (1983), loves houses, cars, planes, and boats. In the 1970s during his earlier TV career, Travolta lived on Woodley Avenue when he played Vinnie Barbarino in the TV series *Welcome Back, Kotter*.

Today his main residence is in Santa Barbara, and he rents in Beverly Hills when filming (at $25,000 a month and more).

Alex Trebek 15

3355 Fryman Road
Studio City, CA 91604

THE HOST OF THE HIT GAME SHOW *JEOPARDY!*, ALEX Trebek, lives on a beautiful two-acre site in the Studio City hills with his wife Jean. Their Fryman Road home, built in 1923 and completely remodeled after their purchase in 1991 for $2,150,000, has twenty-four rooms, including six bedrooms with a lovely pool and garden.

LOT SIZE: **2 ACRES**
HOME SIZE: **9,993 SQ. FT.**
TAXES: **$27,769.54 PER YEAR**

16 Denzel Washington

4701 Sancola Avenue
Toluca Lake, CA 91602

IN THE HEART OF CHARMING TOLUCA LAKE, ON THE EAST side of the San Fernando Valley, charismatic Oscar®-winning actor Denzel Washington, star of *Philadelphia* (1993), *Malcolm X* (1992), and *Glory* (1989), owns a five-bedroom English-style estate with a pool.

Washington purchased this 1940s-era house in 1988 at a reproted price of $1,100,000.

LOT SIZE: 26,998 SQ. FT.
HOME SIZE: 6,063 SQ. FT.

SAN FERNANDO VALLEY

Index

A

ABC Entertainment Center, 93
Abdul, Paula, 37
Academy of Motion Picture Arts and Sciences, 34-35
Albert, Eddie and Margo, 125, 129
Anderson, Pamela, 147, 162
Andrews, Julie, 31, 37, 109
Ann-Margret, 31, 60
Anton, Susan, 31, 62
Arnaz, Desi, 31, 38, 176
Arness, James, 125, 129
Arnold, Tom, 31, 37
Arquette, Rosanna, 15, 19
Astin, John, 91, 96
Azaria, Hank, 15, 19

B

Ball, Lucille, 31, 38, 176
Bancroft, Anne, 139, 142, 147, 154
Bara, Theda, 3, 8-9
Barr, Roseanne, 37, 107, 111
Barrymore, Drew, 3, 10
Bassett, Angela, 3, 10-11
Bates, Kathy, 15, 20
Beachwood, 18
Beatty, Warren, 31, 38, 163
Bel Air, 74-89, 113
Bel Air Hotel, 76-77, 79
Bell, Lauralee, 31, 39, 147, 152
Belushi, James, 107, 112
Berkel, Ron, 35
Berry, Halle, 15, 20
Beverly Hills, 29-73, 128
Beverly Hills Hotel, 32-33, 46, 50, 64
Beverly Park, 57
Boone, Debby, 75, 78
Borgnine, Ernest and Tova, 31, 40
Brando, Marlon, 31, 40
Braxton, Toni, 91, 96
Brentwood, 106-123
Brentwood Country Mart, 110
Brentwood Park, 109-111, 115, 121
Brice, Fanny, 170
Bridges, Jeff, 139, 142, 147, 152
Bridges, Lloyd, 91, 97, 142, 147, 153
Brolin, James, 170
Bronson, Charles, 75, 78, 147, 153
Brooks, Mel, 139, 142, 147, 154
Brunei, Sultan of, 32
Burnett, Carol, 91, 93, 98
Burton, Richard, 88
Buttons, Red and Alicia, 75, 79

C

Caan, James, 75, 79
Cage, Nicolas, 15, 21, 147, 154
Cagney, James, 41
Cain, Dean, 147, 155
Caine, Michael, 31, 41
Cannon, Dyan, 52, 147, 155
Capra, Frank, 71
Carroll, Diahann, 31, 41
Carson, Johnny, 147, 151, 156
Cassidy, Shaun, 31, 42
CBS Television City, 7
Century City, 90-105
Century City Shopping Center, 93
Century Plaza Hotel, 93
Century Towers, 93
Century Woods, 98
Chamberlain, Richard, 39, 64
Chamberlain, Wilt, 75, 80
Chaplin, Charlie, 4, 16, 53
Charisse, Cyd, 31, 42
Charvet, David, 147, 156-157
Chase, Chevy, 125, 130
Checchi, Al, 31, 43
Cher, 147, 157
Chinese Theater. See Mann's Chinese Theater
Clinton, President Bill and Hillary, 35, 128
Coldwater Canyon, 58, 60
Cole, Nat "King," 3, 11
Collins, Gary, 64
Collins, Jackie, 147, 158
Collins, Joan, 31, 43
Collins, Phil, 31, 44
The Colony, 150-151, 155
Cooper, Miriam, 3, 8-9, 9
The Corridor, 92
Cosby, Bill and Camille, 125, 130
Cotten, Joseph, 125, 131
Country Club Park, 5-6
Crawford, Joan, 107, 113, 122
Creative Artists Agency (CAA), 119
Crenna, Richard and Penni, 173, 178
Crosby, Bing and Dixie, 94
Cruise, Tom, 75, 77, 80
Crystal, Billy and Janice, 125, 131
Cummings, Robert, 31, 44
Curtis, Jamie Lee, 139, 143
Curtis, Tony, 33, 143
Curtis-Hall, Vondie, 15, 21

D

Dalton, Timothy, 15, 22
Damone, Vic, 41
Davies, Marion, 18, 31, 45, 141

189

Davis, Marvin, 31, 35-36, 45
Day, Doris, 31, 46
DeMille, Cecil B., 16, 55
Dern, Bruce and Angie, 58, 147, 158
Diamond, Neil, 31, 46
Diller, Phyllis, 107, 113
Disney, Walt, 7
Doheny Mansion, 34
Douglas, Kirk, 31, 47
Douglas, Michael, 107, 114
Dunaway, Faye, 31, 47
Duvall, Robert, 147, 159
Dylan, Bob, 147, 159

E

Eastwood, Clint, 75, 81
Ebsen, Buddy, 3, 12
Edwards, Blake, 37, 109
Eisner, Michael, 57
Encino, 181
Estrada, Erik, 173, 178
Evans, Linda, 31, 48
Evans, Robert, 163

F

Fairbanks, Douglas, Jr., 4, 31-32, 73
Fawcett, Farrah, 75, 81
Field, Ted, 35
Fields, W. C., 4-5
Fisher, Carrie, 31, 49
Fisher, Eddie, 105
Fitzgerald, Ella, 31, 50
Fonda, Henry and Shirlee, 75, 82
Fonda, Peter and Becky, 75, 82
Ford, Glenn, 31, 50
Ford, Harrison, 107, 114
Forsythe, John, 75, 83
Fox, Michael J., 86

G

Gable, Clark, 173, 176, 179
Gabor, Zsa Zsa, 75, 83
Garbo, Greta, 18
Garcia, Andy, 173, 180
Garner, James, 107, 115
Garth, Jennie, 173, 180
Geffen, David, 31, 36, 51
Giannulli, Mossimo, 85
Gillette Regent Square, 140, 144
Gold Coast, 141
Goldman, Ronald, 108
Goldwyn, Sam, 16
Gooding, Cuba, Jr., 173, 181
Gorme, Eydie, 31, 59
Gossett, Louis, Jr., 147, 160
Graham, Heather and Ken, 139, 143
Grant, Cary, 31, 52, 155
Grauman's Chinese Theater. See Mann's

Chinese Theater
Graves, Peter, 129
Greenacres, 35
Gretzky, Wayne, 31, 52-53
Griffith, D. W., 9
Griffith, Melanie, 56

H

Hagman, Larry, 139, 144
Hall, Arsenio, 15, 22
Hamilton, George, 31, 53
The Hamilton House, 112
Hamlin, Harry, 15, 23
Hancock Park, 6-7, 11-12
Hanks, Tom, 107, 115
Harlow, Jean, 31, 54
Harmon, Mark, 109
Harrelson, Woody, 31, 54
Harris, Barbara, 52
Harrison, Rex, 31, 55
Hasselhoff, David, 173, 181
Haver, June, 117
Hawn, Goldie, 125, 132, 147, 160
Hearst, William Randolph, 141
Hefner, Hugh, 91, 94, 99
Hepburn, Audrey, 110
Heston, Charlton, 31, 55
Hollywood, 14-29
Hollywood Hills, 14-29
Hollywoodland, 6, 16
Holmby Hills, 90-105, 113, 170
The Holmes House, 37
Hope, Bob and Dolores, 173, 176, 182
Hopkins, Anthony, 125, 133
Hotel Roosevelt, 17
Houdini, Harry, 16
Hudson, Rock, 31, 56
Hughes, Howard, 7
Humperdinck, Engelbert, 91, 99
Hunt, Helen, 15, 19
Hutton, Barbara, 52

I

Ireland, Jill, 78, 153

J

Jackson, Michael, 147, 161
Jackson family, 110
Johnson, Don, 31, 56
Johnson, Earvin "Magic," Jr., 31, 57
Jones, Quincy, 75, 84
Jones, Tom, 75, 84

K

Karl, Harry, 67
Keaton, Michael, 125, 133
Keith, Brian, 75, 85
Kidman, Nicole, 77, 80

Klugman, Jack, 147, 161
The Knoll, 35-36, 45
Kristofferson, Kris, 147, 162

L

Ladd, Diane, 31, 58
Lamas, Esther Williams, 31, 58
Lamas, Fernando, 57
Lasky, Jesse L., 122
Laughton, Charles, 125, 134
Laurel Canyon, 16, 18-19
Lawrence, Steve, 31, 59
Lear, Norman, 77, 107, 116
Lee, Tommy, 147, 162
Leigh, Janet, 143
Lemmons, Kasi, 15, 21
Leno, Jay and Mavis, 31, 59
Lewis, Thomas, 29
Linden, Hal and Frances, 107, 117
Lithgow, John and Mary, 91, 100
Little Holmby Hills, 92, 97
Lloyd, Harold, 35
Los Angeles, 2-13
Los Angeles Country Club, 59, 67
Los Feliz, 6, 16, 18
Louis, Jean, 29

M

MacGraw, Ali, 147, 163
MacLaine, Shirley, 147, 163
MacMurray, Fred, 107, 117
Madonna, 15, 17, 24, 167
Malibu, 78, 146-171
Malkovich, John, 3, 12
Mancini, Henry and Ginny, 91, 100-101
Mann's Chinese Theater, 17
Mansfield, Jayne, 91, 99
Maps
   Bel Air, 74
   Beverly Hills, 30
   Brentwood, 106
   Century City, 90
   Hollywood, 14
   Hollywood Hills, 14
   Holmby Hills, 90
   Los Angeles, 2
   Malibu (East), 146
   Malibu (West), 148
   Pacific Palisades, 124
   San Fernando Valley (East), 172
   San Fernando Valley (West), 174
   Santa Monica, 138
   West Hollywood, 14
   Westwood, 90
Marina del Rey, 62
Martin, Dean, 31, 60
Martin, Steve, 31, 61
Martin, Tony, 31, 42

Mathison, Melissa, 113
Matthau, Walter and Carol, 125, 134-135, 147, 164
McCarthy, Jenny, 125, 135
McDermott, Dylan, 139, 144
McDowall, Roddy, 173, 183
McGraw, Ali, 107, 118
McMahon, Ed, 31, 61
McQueen, Steve, 107, 110, 118, 163
Medina, Patricia, 130
Mobley, Mary Ann, 64
Monroe, Marilyn, 107, 118-119
Moore, Demi, 31, 72
Moore, Dudley, 31, 62
Mt. Olympus, 21
Mulholland Estates, 37, 52
Murphy, Eddie, 31, 62
Musso & Frank Grill, 18

N

Nelson, Ozzie & Harriet, 15, 24
Newton-John, Olivia, 147, 164
Nichols, Mike, 49
Nicholson, Jack, 31, 63, 147, 165
Nolte, Nick, 147, 165
Novak, Kim, 75, 85

O

O'Brien, Pat, 109
Ocean Park, 140
O'Hara, Maureen, 75, 86
Olsson, Ann-Margaret. See Ann-Margret
O'Neal, Ryan, 75, 81
Outpost Estates, 27
Ovitz, Michael, 107, 119

P

Pacific Palisades, 124-136
Palance, Jack, 31, 64
Palevsky, Max, 68
Palisades Highlands, 130
Palm Springs, 29, 131
Palos Verdes, 12
Paramount Pictures, 7
Parencio, Jerry, 77
The Park, 109-110
Peck, Austin, 91, 101
Peck, Gregory, 107, 109, 120
Penn, Sean, 147, 166
Perry, Matthew, 15, 25
Phillips, Mackenzie, 102
Phillips, Michelle and John, 91, 102
Pickfair, 32, 35, 73
Pickford, Mary, 4, 31-32, 73
Playboy Mansion, 94, 99
Poitier, Sidney, 31, 43
Porter, Cole, 107, 121
Post Office (Beverly Hills), 34

Powers, Stefanie, 31, 64
Presley, Elvis, 31, 60, 65
Presley, Priscilla, 31, 65
Priestley, Jason, 15, 25

R

Rader, Dr. William, 122
Ratzenberger, John, 173, 183
Reagan, President Ronald and Nancy, 77, 127
Reiner, Carl, 31, 66, 121
Reiner, Rob, 107, 121
Reynolds, Burt, 147, 166
Reynolds, Debbie, 31, 67
Richie, Lionel, 75, 86
Riklis, Meshulam, 35, 57, 73
Riordan, Los Angeles Mayor Richard, 113
Riviera Country Club, 109
Robinson, Smokey, 31, 68
Rogers, Kenny, 31, 35-36, 45
Rogers, Will, 126
Ronstadt, Linda, 147, 167
Russell, Kurt, 125, 132

S

Saban, Haim, 57
St. John, Jill, 109, 123
San Fernando Valley, 172-187
Santa Barbara, 61, 142, 186
Santa Monica, 138-145
Santa Ynez Valley, 161
Sassoon, Vidal, 91, 103
Savalas, Telly, 75, 87
Schenck, Joe, 3, 8-9
Schwarzenegger, Arnold, 125, 136
Schwimmer, David, 15, 26
Segal, George, 31, 68-69
Seinfeld, Jerry, 15, 26-27
Selleck, Tom, 91, 103
Sennett, Mack, 8, 16
The Shacker House, 70
Sheen, Martin, 147, 167
Shepherd, Cybill, 173, 184
Shore, Dinah, 31, 69
Shriver, Maria, 125, 136
Shubert Theater, 93
Shue, Andrew and Jennifer, 15, 27
Simpson, Nicole Brown, 107-108, 122
Simpson, O. J., 107-108, 122
Sinatra, Frank, 31, 70, 147, 168
Smart, Jean, 139, 145
Smith, Jaclyn, 75, 87
Snyder, Tom, 31, 70
Spelling, Aaron and Candy, 27, 91, 94, 104, 147, 168
Sprekels, Kay, 179
Stallone, Sylvester, 139, 145, 147, 169
Stevens, Connie, 91, 105

Stewart, Jimmy and Gloria, 31, 71
Stewart, Rod, 39
Stone, Sharon, 15, 28
Streisand, Barbra, 56, 147, 151, 169-170
Struthers, Sally, 107, 113, 122-123
Sullivan Canyon, 109
The Summit, 71
Swayze, Patrick and Lisa Niemi, 173, 184-185

T

Talmadge, Norma, 3-4, 8-9
Taylor, Elizabeth, 75, 88
Thiessen, Tiffani-Amber, 173, 185
Toluca Lake, 180, 187
Travolta, John, 173, 186
Trebek, Alex and Jean, 173, 186
Trousdale Estates, 41-42

W

Wagner, Robert, 107, 109, 123
Walsh, Raoul, 3, 8-9, 9
Warner, Jack, 31, 36, 51
Washington, Denzel, 173, 187
Welk, Lawrence, 125, 137
Welles, Orson, 15, 28
Wendt, George, 147, 171
West, Jerry and Karen, 75, 89
West, Mae, 3-4, 7, 13
West Adams District, 4-7
West Hollywood, 14-29
Westwood, 90-105
Williams, Esther. See Lamas, Esther Williams
Williams, Paul, 95
Willis, Bruce, 31, 72, 147, 171
Will Rogers Ranch, 126
Wilshire Country Club, 13
The Wilshire House, 68, 93
Wilson, Governor Pete, 93
Wilson, Rita, 115
Wilton Place, 6
Windsor Square, 5-6, 12
Wise, Robert, 93
Withers, Grant, 29
Wood, Natalie, 123
Woods, James, 31, 72
Wyans, Damon, 31, 71

Y

Yamashiro Restaurant, 17
Young, Loretta, 15, 29

Z

Zadora, Pia, 31, 35, 73